The Poetry of John Milton

General Editor

C. A. PATRIDES

Professor of English and Related Literature,
University of York

John Milton

Paradise Lost

Books I—II

Introduction by
Philip Brockbank
Professor of English at the University of York

Notes on the Text by
C. A. Patrides

M
MACMILLAN EDUCATION

First published 1972
Reprinted 1975, 1977, 1978, 1979, 1981

Published by
MACMILLAN EDUCATION LIMITED
Houndmills, Basingstoke, Hampshire RG21 2XS
and London
Associated companies in Delhi Dublin
Hong Kong Johannesburg Lagos Melbourne
New York Singapore and Tokyo

Printed in Hong Kong
by China Translation & Printing Services Ltd.

Contents

𝕾𝕾𝕾𝕾𝕾𝕾𝕾𝕾𝕾𝕾𝕾𝕾𝕾𝕾𝕾𝕾𝕾𝕾𝕾𝕾𝕾𝕾𝕾𝕾𝕾𝕾𝕾𝕾𝕾𝕾𝕾𝕾𝕾𝕾𝕾𝕾𝕾𝕾𝕾

Acknowledgements

An edition of Milton's poetry in several volumes necessarily draws on the talents of many critics and scholars, but our primary obligation in this volume is to Professor John T. Shawcross and Doubleday and Co., Inc., for permission to reprint his text from *The Complete English Poetry of John Milton* (New York, 1963). The spelling is here modernised with due regard paid to scansion, unnecessary initial capital letters are reduced and unnecessary italics are eliminated.

The principal contributors to the several volumes were not required to conform to any restrictive guidelines: the introductions were left entirely to their discretion. The notes and the appendices, however, were submitted for their approval.

For general advice I am grateful to J. B. Bamborough, Provost of Linacre College, Oxford; Professor David Daiches of the University of Sussex; and Dame Helen Gardner, Merton Professor of English Literature at Oxford.

I am lastly grateful to the scholars who preceded me as editors of Books I–II—notably M. Y. Hughes (1957), F. T. Prince (1962), and A. D. S. Fowler (1968)—and to Professor Philip Brockbank who provides the introduction to the present volume.

C.A.P.

An Outline
of Milton's Life

Within the context of contemporary events

🙱🙱🙱🙱🙱🙱🙱🙱🙱🙱🙱🙱🙱🙱🙱🙱🙱🙱🙱🙱🙱🙱🙱🙱🙱🙱🙱🙱🙱🙱🙱🙱🙱🙱🙱🙱🙱🙱🙱

The Reign of James I

1603 24 Mar: death of Elizabeth I; accession of James I
1608 9 Dec: John Milton born in Bread Street, Cheapside, London
1612 Death of Henry, Prince of Wales
1616 Death of Shakespeare
1618 Execution of Sir Walter Ralegh
1620 Settlement of first New England colony by the Pilgrim Fathers
1620? Milton attends St Paul's School (to 1924)
1621 Andrew Marvell born
1625 12 Feb: Milton admitted to Christ's College, Cambridge;
        matriculated on 9 April
        27 Mar: death of James I; accession of Charles I

The Reign of Charles I

1625 Outbreak of the plague
1626 Death of Sir Francis Bacon
1629 26 Mar: Milton admitted to the Degree of Bachelor of Arts
1630 Prince Charles (later Charles II) born
1631 Death of John Donne
1632 3 July: Milton admitted to the Degree of Master of Arts.
        His poem 'On Shakespeare' published in the Second Folio
        of Shakespeare's plays. Resides at Hammersmith with
        family (to 1635?)

1633 William Laud appointed Archbishop; demands conformity against mounting opposition

1634 29 Sept: *A Mask* [*Comus*] performed

1635? Milton resides at Horton, Buckinghamshire, with family (to 1638)

1637 *A Mask* [*Comus*] published
      3 April: death of Milton's mother
      Death of Ben Jonson

1638 *Lycidas* published in a memorial volume to Edward King
      April (?): Milton embarks on a visit to France and Italy

1639 War with Scotland
      Milton returns to London in the late summer, tutors privately (to about 1647); resides first at St Bride's Churchyard, then at Aldersgate Street (to 1645)

1641 The Long Parliament convenes
      Laud is impeached and imprisoned
      Milton engaged in the war of the pamphlets concerning the episcopal form of ecclesiastical government; his five anti-prelatical tracts begin with *Of Reformation*, probably in May; *Of Prelatical Episcopy*, in June or July; and *Animadversions*, in July
      Execution of Strafford
      Irish Rebellion
      The 'Grand Remonstrance' issued

1642 Milton publishes two more anti-prelatical tracts, *The Reason of Church Government*, in January or February, and *An Apology*, in April
      Parliamentary strength increases; Charles I removes to Oxford
      June (?): Milton marries Mary Powell; she returns to her father's home, probably in August
      22 Aug: Charles I raises his standard at Nottingham; the Civil War begins

1643 'Solemn League and Covenant': Parliament undertakes to reform the church

1 Aug: Milton publishes the first of four divorce tracts, *The Doctrine and Discipline of Divorce*

1644 Parliamentary victory at Marston Moor

Milton publishes *Of Education* in June, and *Areopagitica* in November; the second divorce tract, *The Judgement of Martin Bucer*, published in August

1645 Execution of Laud

Rise of the New Model Army; Parliamentary victories at Naseby and elsewhere

March: Milton publishes the last two divorce tracts, *Tetrachordon* and *Colasterion*

Summer (?): Mary Powell returns to Milton; they reside at Barbican (to 1647)

Dec: (?): 1st edition of *The Poems of Mr John Milton* ('The Minor Poems')

1646 29 July: birth of Milton's first daughter Anne

1647 13 Mar (?): death of Milton's father

Aug: Parliamentary army occupies London

Milton resides at High Holborn (to 1649)

Charles I is arrested; escapes

1648 Second Civil War; Charles I is seized

25 Aug: birth of Milton's second daughter Mary

1649 30 Jan: execution of Charles I

Charles II, proclaimed in Scotland, escapes to France in 1651

The Interregnum

1649 Feb: Milton endorses regicide in *The Tenure of Kings and Magistrates*

15 Mar: Milton appointed Secretary of Foreign Tongues to the Council of State (to 1659?); resides first at Charing Cross, then at Scotland Yard, Westminster (to 1651)

Cromwell in Ireland

Oct: Milton at the order of the Council of State writes and publishes *Eikonoklastes* ('The Image Breaker') in reply to *Eikon Basilike* ('The Royal Image'), attributed to Charles I

1650   Milton issues enlarged editions of *The Tenure of Kings and Magistrates* and *Eikonoklastes*

His blindness progresses rapidly

1651   Feb: Milton at the order of the Council of States writes and publishes *Pro populo anglicano defensio* (the so-called 'First Defence of the English People') in reply to Salmasius's defence of Charles I (1649)

16 Mar: birth of Milton's first son John; the family move to Petty France, Westminster (to 1660)

Hobbes's *Leviathan* published

1652   End of war in Ireland

Milton's blindness becomes total

2 May: birth of Milton's third daughter Deborah

5 May (?): death of his wife Mary

15 June (?): death of his son John

1653   The Protectorate established under Cromwell

1654   May: Milton at the order of the Council of State writes and publishes *Defensio secunda pro populo anglicano* ('The Second Defence of the English People') in reply to Pierre du Moulin's attack on the Commonwealth (1652)

1655   Aug: Milton publishes *Pro se defensio* ('Defence of Himself') in reply to a personal attack by Alexander More (1654)

1656   12 Nov: Milton marries Katherine Woodcock

1657   Sept (?): Andrew Marvell appointed Milton's assistant in the Secretaryship

19 Oct: birth of Milton's fourth daughter Katherine

1658   3 Feb: death of Milton's second wife Katherine

17 Mar: death of his daughter Katherine

3 Sept: death of Cromwell; the Protectorate passes to his son Richard

1659   Milton publishes *A Treatise of Civil Power* in February, and

  Considerations touching the likeliest means to remove Hirelings
  out of the Church in August

  25 May: Richard Cromwell obliged to abdicate; the Pro-
  tectorate ends

1660 Feb: Milton publishes *The Ready and Easy Way to Establish*
  a Free Commonwealth

  29 May: Charles II, recalled by Parliament, enters London

The Restoration

1660 Milton imprisoned for a time; copies of his books burned by
  order of Parliament

  The theatres, closed since 1642, re-opened

  The Royal Society founded

1661 Milton after a brief stay at Holborn, resides at Jewin Street
  (to 1663)

1662 'Act of Uniformity'

1663 24 Feb: Milton marries Elizabeth Minshull; they reside at
  Artillery Walk, Bunhill Fields (to 1674)

1664 Autumn: outbreak of the Great Plague; Milton moves
  temporarily to Chalfont St Giles, Bucks.

1666 Sept: London devastated by fire

1667 Aug (?): *Paradise Lost* published

1669 June (?): Milton's *Accidence Commenc't Grammar* published

1670 Nov (?): Milton's *History of Britain* published

1671 Feb (?): *Paradise Regained* and *Samson Agonistes* published
  jointly (2nd edition, posthumously in 1680)

1672 May (?): Milton's *Artis Logicae Plenior Institutio* ('A Fuller
  Institution of the Art of Logic') published

1673 May (?): Milton's *Of True Religion, Heresy, Schism and*
  Toleration published

  Nov (?): 2nd enlarged edition of the 'Minor Poems' (1645)

1674 May: Milton's *Epistolae Familiares et Prolusiones* ('Letters and
  Prolusions') published

  July: 2nd revised edition of *Paradise Lost*

Death of Milton about 8 November; buried in St Giles, Cripplegate, on 12 November

Milton's posthumously published works include in particular his Latin treatise on Christian doctrine, *De Doctrina Christiana* (discovered in 1823, first published in 1825).

Introduction

🕮🕮🕮🕮🕮🕮🕮🕮🕮🕮🕮🕮🕮🕮🕮🕮🕮🕮🕮🕮🕮🕮🕮🕮🕮🕮🕮🕮🕮🕮🕮🕮🕮🕮

When other poets of the seventeenth century (Henry Vaughan,
for example, and Richard Crashaw) wrote about the birth of Christ,
they sang with the shepherds; but Milton sang with the angels.
In the great hymn, *On the Morning of Christ's Nativity*, the human
world and the natural (wind, water and stars) are subdued to stillness
by the 'divinely warbled voice' that we recognise as Milton's own:

> Ring out ye crystal spheres,
> Once bless our human ears,
>   (If ye have power to touch our senses so)
> And let your silver chime
> Move in melodious time;
>   And let the base of heav'n's deep organ blow,
> And with your ninefold harmony
> Make up full consort to th' angelic symphony.
>
> For if such holy song
> Enwrap our fancy long,
>   Time will run back, and fetch the age of gold,
> And speckl'd vanity
> Will sicken soon and die,
>   And leprous sin will melt from earthly mould,
> And hell itself will pass away,
> And leave her dolorous mansions to the peering day.
>
> (125–40)

By the end of the poem that incantatory melody of verse has, in the
poet's imagination, quieted nature, brought peace to earth and good-
will to men, held the turning spheres to a more reverend motion,

and announced the return of the golden age. Milton, like Orpheus and like the David of the Psalms, has cast a spell, and it is our privilege to be delighted and entranced by an excitement and prospect satisfying at once to our physical and to our moral senses.

Milton was pre-eminently a formidable enchanter. As a pamphleteer as well as a poet, he sought to be a commanding and Olympian voice, and where others might address themselves to 'all Englishmen', he would astonish the whole of Europe:

> I imagine myself not in the forum or on the rostra, surrounded only by the people of Athens or of Rome; but about to address in this as I did in my former defence, the whole collective body of people, cities, states, and councils of the wise and eminent, through the wide expanse of anxious and listening Europe. I seem to survey as from a towering height, the far extended tracts of sea and land, and innumerable crowds of spectators, betraying in their looks the liveliest interest, and sensations the most congenial with my own.[1]

The language that seeks to dominate so vast an audience to such ambitious ends must, like the incantatory Orphic song, seek to carry us into orbit by the energies of its flight.

It is not surprising that Milton's aspirations and abilities have won for him an answering kind of commendation. 'He can occasionally invest himself with grace,' says Dr Johnson, 'but his natural port is gigantic loftiness. He can please when pleasure is required; but it is his peculiar power to astonish.' Nor is it surprising that such commendation should be attended by misgivings—the towering heights are only attained by those who in some measure bid farewell to their ordinary humanity, and hold themselves remote from intimacies of observation and feeling. However, although in the end we may

[1] *The Second Defence of the People of England* (1654), translated from Milton's Latin by Robert Fellowes

wish to make that kind of qualification, we must recognise that Milton himself believed there was no necessary distance between the more austere and the more tender vitalities of language. The poet's abilities, he proclaimed, 'are the inspired gift of God ... to imbreed and cherish in a great people the seeds of virtue and public civility, to allay the perturbations of the mind, and set the affections in right tune.' These resonant phrases are from one of Milton's earliest pamphlets, *The Reason of Church Government*, and they are part of his response to the issues of the imminent civil war. They will often serve to describe the endeavour of his art.

Revolution, Paradise, and the Fall

'I can hardly refrain', says Milton in his *Second Defence*, 'from assuming a more lofty and swelling tone ... and much as I may be surpassed by the powers of eloquence, and copiousness of diction, by the illustrious orators of antiquity; yet the subject of which I treat was never surpassed in any age, in dignity or interest.' That subject was the judicial execution of King Charles I, and Milton (writing in Latin in emulation of Cicero upon the death of Caesar) is the clarion voice of triumphant revolution.

Milton's role in the civil war was conspicuous and momentous; although he did not bear arms he was for twenty years a vehement and prolific advocate of revolutionary moderation. 'Most poets', he observes, 'have been the strenuous enemies of despotisms', and both as poet and as orator he fought to free England from the despotisms of Episcopacy and Monarchy in the territories of spiritual and civil liberty. By spiritual liberty he meant the freedom of every man to seek his own salvation by interpreting the scripture to 'his own best light, which God hath planted in him to that purpose'. This freedom had for many years been abrogated and frustrated by the cruelly enforced hieratic policies of Archbishop Laud. As for civil liberty, the King by 1640 had ruled eleven years without a parliament, and there had grown up about him a proliferation of claims to divine and immutable right.

Milton was a revolutionary in believing that by 1642 the King and the established leaders of the Church had left the 'people of England' no choice but the exercise of force. He was a moderate in that he moved between the authoritarian positions and the anarchic. He consistently resisted any attribution of human power to divine sanction: 'To say kings are accountable to none but God', he wrote, 'is the overturning of all law and government', and, 'The power of kings and magistrates is only derivative, transferred and committed to them in trust from the people to the common good of them all.' But he had no confidence either in the spontaneous and natural community of equals advocated by the 'Diggers' or 'True Levellers'. He believed in government by the few in the service of the many, in obedience to the authorities of conscience and scripture. Power should be held on trust and exercised with responsibility, but under Charles and his bishops the power had been abused, the responsibility neglected and the trust forfeited.

The letters that Milton wrote to foreign governments during the ten years he served as Latin secretary to Cromwell and to Parliament exhibit many of the qualities usually associated with the moderate position—the sweet reasonableness, the readiness to compromise, the affected diffidence, the diplomatic turn of phrase. But these are rarely to be found in his polemical writings. There, on the contrary, he is often venomous and intolerant, making mock of the liturgy ('still serving to all the abominations of the antichristian temple'), and abusing some of the greatest scholars of Europe (he called one, in Latin, a tumid pumpkin and a pragmatical puppy). Much of the intolerance, however, can be set down to the conventions of political and ecclesiastical dispute, which in the seventeenth century encouraged extravagance and hyperbole on all sides. Throughout the achievements and disappointments of the revolution, Milton's central, moderate convictions about the nature of government remained unchanged. Even in the confusion that followed the collapse of the commonwealth under Richard Cromwell in 1659, he could still argue that 'the basis of every just and free government . . . is a general council of ablest men, chosen by the people to consult of public affairs from time to time for the common good.'

But from the moderate practice of government Milton often had immoderate and apocalyptic expectations—as if an access of political, spiritual and domestic freedom would bring into being a marvellously satisfying, perhaps paradisal, state of society. It is in the promises and frustrations of this idea over the years 1640 to 1660 that we might perceive the need that Milton found to write *Paradise Lost*. Characteristically, Milton in several of his pamphlets extends his thinking from the state of the realm in the sixteen-forties to the human condition since the fall of man in the garden of Eden, and so did many of his contemporaries. The story of Adam and Eve came to have much importance for several kinds of political thinker in the seventeenth century, but the question 'Is it true?' which was to matter so much to the Christian disputants who confronted Darwin in the nineteenth century, was of far less consequence than the question, 'What truth does it convey?' The story (or myth) conjoins the auspicious truths about man—the privilege of his intelligence, and his free inheritance of the bounty of the earth, with the inauspicious—his long history of internecine violence, exploitation and squalor. To read the riddle of the fall—the fruit, the serpent, the expulsion—might be to find the key to the recovery of the naturally paradisal state of man.

It would not be appropriate to attempt to review all the views that were entertained in seventeenth-century England, but it may be of help to notice that interpretations very different from Milton's were offered on what we would now (ineptly) call the platforms of the political 'left' and 'right'. For Gerrard Winstanley, the Christian communist and 'Digger', the fall of Adam and Eve was owed to the serpent's seductive power over their imaginations, creating illusions of self-fulfilment and self-assertion that precipitated the evil human passion for dominion over others. If men were again attentive (like the unfallen Adam) to the voice of God within, all men would with equal delight, in love and in reason, recover their paradisal heritage. The fall was for Winstanley, not a specific event in the remote past, but a present truth about how men behave, about the hell they create for themselves and the heaven they deny themselves, when they are moved by impulses other than love and reason. His vision can be both demonstratively and ironically illustrated by the heroic but pitiful history of his own movement. Over a period of several months in 1649, he and a few followers (sometimes three or four, sometimes fifty) cultivated and farmed St George's Hill near Cobham in Surrey, pleading that it was common land and belonged to the common people. By sharing their labour and their produce they hoped to 'restore creation' and make the earth a 'common treasury of livelihood to whole mankind, without respect of persons'. Mankind, however, responded either with indifference (although two other Digger colonies were started) or with ruthless hostility. Mobs attacked and beat them, broke their spades, burned their houses, clubbed their cattle and dug up their corn. Winstanley and his followers endured cheerfully and patiently (for was not Jesus Christ 'the head Leveller'?), but by the summer of 1650 the movement was discouraged and exhausted.

Those newspaper editors who troubled to comment at the time were apt, in sympathy or in mockery, to make their points by allusion to the fall: 'these men were begotten as frogs . . . had they been of Adam, they had had passions, and then of necessity laws'. Laws and property were the necessary evils attendant upon the fall. Winstanley's version of the fall confronts this argument with a different assumption about human nature: if men were freed from political and economic servitude they would in freedom recover their divine humanity. Men must be given the chance. But from the myth of the fall the retort might be, 'man was given a chance, and he made a mess of it'; and from the history of mankind we know of many chances and many messes—including those which the revolution offered in Milton's and Cromwell's England.

One of the more pessimistic spectators to the revolution, who might be taken to represent a view of human nature quite contrary to Winstanley's, was Thomas Hobbes. Hobbes moved in fear of what would become of mankind if all were to listen to their inner voices. By his account, the impulses that move men when they are free from all constraints are self-seeking, aggressive and murderous, and he would therefore be less surprised than the Diggers by the cruel mobs upon St George's Hill. The story of Adam and Eve shows, according to Hobbes, that obedience was the first and principal virtue, and that disobedience was (and is) the radical cause of man's fall from grace. Hobbes offers no hope of recovery of the paradisal state, however, and finds it significant that once Adam had tasted of the tree of the knowledge of good and evil, he could taste no more of the tree of life—he fell into the mortal condition. Men can only hope to make the best of their inescapably fallen and imperfect condition by honouring the 'contract' that Hobbes postulates between rulers and ruled: so long as its governors are protecting society from lapsing into anarchy and chaos, the governed are under an obligation to obey them.

Milton as a political thinker was more sceptical than Winstanley and more visionary than Hobbes. In a pamphlet of 1648, one of several in defence of the regicide, he writes:

> No man, who knows aught, can be so stupid to deny, that all men naturally were born free, being the image and resemblance of God himself, and were, by privilege above all the creatures, born to command, and not to obey: and that they lived so, till from the root of Adam's transgression, falling among themselves to do wrong and violence, and foreseeing that such courses must needs tend to the destruction of them all, they agreed by common league to bind each other from mutual injury, and jointly to defend themselves against any, that gave disturbance or opposition to such agreement. Hence came cities, towns and commonwealths. And because no faith in all was

found sufficiently binding, they saw it needful to ordain some
authority, that might restrain by force and punishment what was
violated against peace and common right.[1]

The reflection that 'no faith in all was found sufficiently binding'
might have dismayed Winstanley, and Milton's version of a contract
might, with some differences of emphasis, have been endorsed by
Hobbes. But Milton cares more than Hobbes for 'common league',
'common right', and mutuality, and had better hope that human
freedom could be creatively exercised in the fallen world. This hope
was severely tested in the later years of the commonwealth, as the
authority of Parliament was menaced on the one hand by popular
agitation and on the other by the assumption of personal power by
Cromwell.

In the *Second Defence* Milton fears the blight of democratic faction,
of power falling into the hands of those 'who think that they can
never be free, till the liberties of others depend upon their caprice'.
The revolution, from Milton's point of view, was in danger of
betraying its magnanimous intentions to the tyranny of a mob that
came 'reeking from the taverns and the stews' to dictate to parlia-
ment by 'clamour and intimidation'. Those who cannot rule them-
selves must not rule the country—therefore Milton exhorted the
people to deserve their freedom better:

> For it is of no little consequence, O citizens, by what principles
> you are governed, either in acquiring liberty, or in retaining it
> when acquired. And unless that liberty, which is of such a kind
> as arms can neither procure nor take away, which alone is the
> fruit of piety, of justice, of temperance and unadulterated virtue,
> shall have taken deep root in your minds and hearts, there will
> not be wanting one who will snatch from you by treachery
> what you have acquired by arms. War has made many great
> whom peace makes small.

[1] *The Tenure of Kings and Magistrates* (1648)

After the triumphs of the battlefield there waits, if temptations go
unresisted, the ready 'fall' into the 'abyss' of corruption; the Puritans
may be contaminated, Milton fears, by the habits and attitudes of
Cavaliers. The fall and redemption from it are not social experiences
only, but profoundly personal, and personal failures have immense
social and even cosmic consequences.

Despite its sombre and apprehensive moments, however, the
Second Defence makes its affirmations, as Milton recovers from his
misgivings and eagerly anticipates the full emancipation of a people
who through obedience to reason will in time learn to govern
themselves. He compares himself to an 'epic poet' who has 'heroic-
ally celebrated at least one exploit of his countrymen', and hopes
still that what was gloriously begun might be gloriously ended, in
the creation of a community that would be the envy of the world.
These themes, much changed, distanced, complicated and enriched,
will be resumed by Milton when he is indeed, and not by analogy,
the epic poet addressing himself to mankind at large.

The Epic of 'Paradise Lost'

While it is good to remember that *Paradise Lost* was shaped by the
political experience of seventeenth-century England and Europe, it is
also good to forget. For while the period was remarkable for its
creative accomplishments in music, literature and philosophy, it
was also one of the cruellest in history, leaving the rival idealisms
of Christendom almost totally exhausted by stupid, cataclysmic
violence. From the Thirty Years' War to the War of the Spanish
Succession the scale of holocausts is frightening even now. Milton
could speak of 'the rebellion and horrid massacre of English pro-
testants in Ireland, to the number of 154,000 in the province of
Ulster only, by their own computation'; eight years later, recovering
Ireland for the Protestant cause, Cromwell had all but one of the

garrison of 3000 at Drogheda killed, and could write, 'truly I believe this bitterness will save much effusion of blood, through the goodness of God', to justify his measures to the Council of State.

It was vital for Milton that events should be seen in a perspective more generous than the mean one afforded by contemporary history. This, for Milton as for others, was provided by the literary traditions of ancient Greece and Rome, of the Hebrew Bible, and of renaissance Italy. Literary traditions are of course related to the civilisations from which they grow, and therefore to the history of those civilisations, but they are richer and ampler than the historical record. Through the fullest resources of language they express and conserve (some would say 'eternalise') experiences, aspirations and insights that may leave few traces in the debris of historical fact. So it is with the Homeric wars and with the exodus of the Jews, with Shakespeare's Wars of the Roses and with the Irish events of 1916 to 1919 in the poetry of Yeats.

Milton's knowledge of the literature of Europe was exceptionally spacious, and it was not merely passive; he saw himself as heir to Homer, to the prophet Isaiah, to Virgil and to Dante. He meant with *Paradise Lost* to endow English civilisation and the English language with a masterpiece of epic art. Milton had had an early ambition of the kind when he resolved (he tells us in 1642) 'to fix all the art and industry I could unite to the adorning of my native tongue; not to make verbal curiosities the end, (that were a toilsome vanity,) but to be an interpreter and relater of the best and sagest things among mine own citizens throughout this island in the mother dialect.' And in the Latin poem *Mansus* (1638) he hopes that someday he may commemorate the deeds of King Arthur in heroic song. The projected *Arthuriad*, as it is sometimes called, would have been pre-eminently a patriotic battle poem 'proclaiming the magnanimous heroes of the invincible table', and it might have offered interludes for relating 'the best and sagest things' that their discourse offered. But such an undertaking, while it might catch the imagination of the thirty-year-old poet four years before the outbreak of the civil war,

would look culpably innocent to the mature Milton who began
work on his epic at some point between 1655 and 1658.

No man at the centre of events could at that time put unequivocal
faith in the simple heroic virtues. A note most ominous for heroic
causes had already been sounded in the passage quoted here on page
20 from the *Second Defence*: 'War has made many great whom peace
makes small.' In Book XI of *Paradise Lost*, Adam will muse upon the
spectacle of disappointments and disasters that Michael foresees for
mankind:

> I had hope
> When violence was ceas'd, and war on earth,
> All would have then gone well, peace would have crown'd
> With length of happy days the race of man;
> But I was far deceiv'd; for now I see
> Peace to corrupt no less then war to waste.
>
> (XI, 779–84)

Some reflection on this and other passages from Book XI will suggest
the closeness and the distance of the poem to Milton's experience as
a Puritan revolutionary. *Paradise Lost* does not 'indite wars':

> hitherto the only argument
> Heroic deem'd, chief mastery to dissect
> With long and tedious havoc fabl'd knights
> In battles feign'd;
>
> (IX, 28–31)

It seeks rather to endue the Puritan cause with a richer spiritual and
imaginative life, one which (to recall *The Reason of Church Govern-
ment*) 'allayed the perturbations of the mind, and set the affections
in right tune'.

We need phrases like these to remind us of the profound differences
that underlie the many resemblances between the motives of Milton's
poetry and those of his pamphlets. Poetry can enrich the content
of belief in ways that are beyond the resources of polemical prose.

It touches our senses more intimately and it changes relation-
ships between the feelings that we are content to rest in, and the
convictions that we hope to put into operation, between our images
of ideal arrival and our dispositions to move in the right direction.
Poetry must, by Milton's account, be 'simple, sensuous and passion-
ate', and yet 'fraught with an universal insight into things'. These are
mysterious claims to make, and to vindicate them we must look
more closely at Milton's art.

Celestial Song

The opening lines of *Paradise Lost* are at once daunting and exhilara-
ting; daunting, because the movement of the verse alights so inexor-
ably on 'disobedience', 'forbidden', 'mortal', 'death' and 'woe';
exhilarating because the verb, so long withheld, comes at last in a
proud invocation ('Sing heav'nly Muse') breathlessly sustained
through a sentence of sixteen lines. It is a triumph of expressive
rhythm and syntax that seems effacingly to claim that Milton has
mastered at once the moral order of creation and the creative arts
of the poet's song. The impression is apt enough, for here (as at the
start of Books VII and IX) the 'heav'nly Muse' invoked is Urania,
who first taught Moses about creation and who existed (as we learn
from Book VII) 'Before the hills appear'd, or fountains flow'd':

> Thou with eternal Wisdom didst converse,
> Wisdom thy sister, and with her didst play
> In presence of th' almighty Father, pleas'd
> With thy celestial song.

Milton is remembering the eighth chapter of Proverbs which tells
that Wisdom was present when God first ordered the world and
'set a compass upon the face of the depth'. But by making Urania
converse and play with Sophia (Wisdom) to the delight of God the
Father, Milton is finding in religious and poetical language a way of
claiming that the ultimate principles by which the cosmic order
comes into being are both moral (the 'eternal wisdom') and aesthetic

(the 'celestial song'). It is possible to believe otherwise—that creation
is fortuitous, for example, or obedient to merely mechanical laws,
or to some amoral vital energy. But Milton gives precedence to the
moral and aesthetic impulses both in the processes of natural creation
and in his creative art. So do all poets, it might be said; but Milton
would reach beyond the merely human world and beyond merely
human understanding—he would 'justify the ways of God to man',
and he would pursue 'Things unattempted yet in prose or rhyme.'
He would expound eternal wisdom and imitate the celestial song.

Celestial song is remote from common speech, and Dr Johnson
rightly said that 'an unlearned reader, when he first opens his book,
finds himself surprised by a new language'. Many have shared
Johnson's exasperated wonder. He was not appeased by those who
impute the novelty of Milton's 'Babylonish dialect' to his 'laborious
endeavours after words suitable for the grandeur of his ideas', and
thought that both in prose and verse his style was formed 'by a
perverse and pedantic principle'. Nevertheless, he says, 'such is the
power of his poetry, that his call is obeyed without resistance, the
reader feels himself in captivity to a higher and nobler mind, and
criticism sinks in admiration.' This may be looked upon as the
response that Milton (himself captive to a higher voice) hoped for.
But there are readers less ready to submit. 'Reading *Paradise Lost*', says
Dr F. R. Leavis, 'is a matter of resisting, of standing up against, the
verse-movement, of subduing it into something tolerably like sensi-
tiveness, and in the end our resistance is worn down; we surrender
at last to the inescapable monotony of the ritual.'

The call obeyed without resistance, the captivity to a higher and
nobler mind, and the surrender to the inescapable monotony of the
ritual, are all ways of acknowledging the incantatory spell of the
poem. Spells are not always efficacious, wings may beat without
flight, and the muses may not come when they are called. How is the
spell cast, and to what ends? Is there one spell, or are there many?
'Milton's style', says Johnson, 'was not modified by his subject:
what is shown with greater extent in *Paradise Lost*, may be found in

Comus'. In a sense it is so. Before attempting to discriminate the 'answerable style' that Milton hoped for from his 'celestial patroness', Urania, we can with advantage glance back to the earlier poems.

Many readers have attempted to measure the distances between Milton and Shakespeare, and in a little poem prefaced to Shakespeare's second Folio, Milton himself offers some of the useful phrases. Where Shakespeare's 'easy numbers flow' (a common conviction at the time) his is a 'slow-endeavouring art'; and in an exquisitely mysterious and equivocal compliment, Milton bids farewell to an inspiration that is inimitable and dead:

> Then thou our fancy of itself bereaving,
> Dost make us marble with too much conceiving.

Shakespeare's monument is in his work and in our awed response to it; but he has also exhausted the admiring imagination of Milton and turned him to stone, making Milton's art 'marble with too much conceiving'.

Milton could not emulate Shakespeare but tried to find other energies in the language, and other forms in which to express his genius. He found his opportunity largely in hymns, psalms and elegies (in English and Latin) on models (classical, Hebrew or Italian) that Shakespeare had not enlisted. One strain, already observed, was the inspiration of incantatory 'melodious noise' (the phrase is from *At a Solemn Music*), meant like the songs of David and Orpheus to 'keep in tune with heav'n'. Through it, Milton taught the language a greater resonance, and cultivated the 'God-gifted organ voice' that Tennyson commended. This is the strain that becomes the 'celestial song' of Urania in *Paradise Lost*.

But in the early poetry we can detect other related strains too. In *Lycidas*, for example, Milton pushes his language and his themes away from terrestrial and mortal things towards some imagined timeless world first made out of, and then dissociated from, the actual mutable world in which things die and turn sour. Strange things happen to words—the Babylonish dialect is in the making:

> Throw hither all your quaint enamell'd eyes
> That on the green turf suck the honied show'rs
> And purple all the ground with vernal flow'rs.
>
> (139–41)

If we ask, how can eyes be enamelled? and how can they suck showers? we are silenced by the invincible tempo of the incantation, and consoled with the elusive impression of flowers shaped like eyes, intensely coloured and taking rain from the earth. The surrealism of 'enamell'd eyes' is perhaps assisted by the uncertain syntax, for we may be tricked in passing into supposing 'eyes' the subject of the adjectival verb 'purple'.

A less extreme instance of this de-actualising process may be found in the celebrated lines:

> Fame is the spur that the clear spirit doth raise
> (That last infirmity of noble mind)
> To scorn delights, and live laborious days;
>
> (70–2)

Glancing back to Shakespeare, we may recall from *Macbeth*,

> I have no spur
> To prick the sides of my intent, but only
> Vaulting ambition, which o'erleaps itself,
> And falls on the other.

and make comparison of the two spurs. Shakespeare needs the concrete connotation, the rider and the horse with sides to prick. But Milton needs the abstract. 'Spur' in *Lycidas* means 'incitement' and has lost its immediate energy. The metaphor is extraordinarily attenuated and seems meant to be so, clarifying a remote and timeless moral endeavour.

Behind *Lycidas* is the will to transfigure sense-experience and personal emotion (Johnson was right to say there is no nature in the poem and no grief) in a death-transcending world of verbal art. This impulse might fairly be called 'neo-platonic'. Like Plato, Milton puts a comparatively low value on the world of the senses and aspires to an order beyond it; but where Plato allows to the artist only the ability to copy mundane realities, Milton like many of Plato's later followers would allow him to pre-figure ideal realities.

When Yeats was trying to find for himself a poet's role in the Irish civil war, he bought himself a symbolic tower, and he remembered Milton:

> *Il Penseroso's* Platonist toiled on
> In some like chamber, shadowing forth
> How the daemonic rage
> Imagined everything.

He had in mind the passage where Milton asks that 'his lamp at midnight hour/Be seen in some high lonely tower', and hopes to

> unsphere
> The spirit of the Plato to unfold
> What worlds, or what vast regions hold
> Th' immortal mind that hath forsook
> Her mansion in this fleshly nook:
> And of those daemons that are found
> In fire, air, flood, or under ground,
> Whose power hath a true consent
> With planet, or with element.
>
> (88–96)

Fantastically, we may think, Milton's Platonist, forsaking the flesh and dedicated to the scholar's toil, is credited with a daemonic power to master all the secrets of creation and bring it under his control. *Il Penseroso* is a playful literary exercise, but like Marlowe before him and like Yeats after, Milton has cosmic ambitions; he would see human life as an astronomical as well as social spectacle.

Early in Book IX, approaching the climax of the poem when Eve tastes of the apple, Milton will rise to the occasion if he can be properly inspired:

> If answerable style I can obtain
> Of my celestial patroness, who deigns
> Her nightly visitation unimplor'd,
> And dictates to me slumb'ring, or inspires
> Easy my unpremeditated verse:
>
> (IX, 20–4)

It is surprising that after the formulation ('answerable style'), the stiffness ('obtain', 'deigns') and the weight, there is (after the crucial word 'inspires') that liberated flow and tumble of syllables into the last line—'Easy my unpremeditated verse'. Effects of release from constraint and effects of flight are characteristic of Milton's power to move us, and they are often won by control of rhythm, cadence and pace. It is significant here that the effect conveys Milton's confidence in his more spontaneous writing—that which, we might say by a different metaphor, wells up from the unconscious. While he thought of the poet's trade as arduous ('strictly meditate the thankless muse'), it is clear that long practice in his own poetic dialect had made it often subliminal and spontaneous.

The most felicitous of all commendations of Milton's Uranian language is Andrew Marvell's in his prefatory poem:

> Thou singst with so much gravity and ease;
> And above human flight dost soar aloft
> With plume so strong, so equal and so soft.
> The bird nam'd from that Paradise you sing
> So never flags, but always keeps on wing.

It is well said; but we must not allow it to deceive us into supposing the poem always in flight. The unflagging quality of *Paradise Lost* is not always soaring, but makes itself felt as a rigorous effort to

keep going. After setting aside the traditional martial themes that
give 'heroic name /To person or to poem', Milton laboriously muses:

> Me of these
> Nor skill'd nor studious, higher argument
> Remains, sufficient of itself to raise
> That name, unless an age too late, or cold
> Climate, or years damp my intended wing
> Depress'd, and much they may, if all be mine,
> Not hers who brings it nightly to my ear.
>
> (IX, 41–7)

This is one of many passages that might prompt us to say that the
poem is sustained both by an aethereal impulse, an eagerness to
move freely in words through time and space; and an ascetic one,
a readiness to endure the ordeals of mortality and to submit to an
exacting moral law. Another such passage is found early in Book VII:

> Half yet remains unsung but narrower bound
> Within the visible diurnal sphere;
> Standing on earth, not rapt above the pole,
> More safe I sing with mortal voice, unchang'd
> To hoarse or mute, though fall'n on evil days,
> On evil days though fall'n, and evil tongues;
> In darkness, and with dangers compass'd round,
> And solitude; yet not alone, while thou
> Visit'st my slumbers nightly, or when morn
> Purples the east: still govern thou my song,
> Urania, and fit audience find, though few.
> But drive far off the barbarous dissonance
> Of Bacchus and his revellers, the race
> Of that wild rout that tore the Thracian bard
> In Rhodope, where woods and rocks had ears
> To rapture, till the savage clamour drown'd

> Both harp and voice; nor could the Muse defend
> Her son. So fail not thou, who thee implores:
> For thou art heav'nly, she an empty dream.
>   (VII, 21–39)

There are many reasons for recalling these lines, at once the most personal and the most comprehensive expression of Milton's ecstasy and anguish; it may be to notice that the Thracian bard is the Orpheus of *Lycidas*, or that the dissonance of the revellers has been heard before in *Comus* and will again in *Samson Agonistes*. But primarily, it is to observe the blind poet confronting a hostile regime and a barbarous London (the revellers of the Restoration streets and the murderous mobs) with an appropriate serenity and an appropriate moral ferocity.

In *Comus*, the Lady, assisted by her own integrity, her brothers' vigilance and the solicitude of the Attendant Spirit, survives the ordeal of the wood to enjoy a prospect of sensual and spiritual rapture. The virtues she must exercise in the wood are of the negative, rigorous, temptation-resisting kind. The poet, we may say (adapting what Keats said of Shakespeare) lives a life of allegory and his works are the comment on it. Milton 'in darkness, and with dangers compass'd round', yet singing—'rapt above the pole' or in mortal voice 'Within the visible diurnal sphere', is undergoing a pilgrimage similar to the Lady's.

While the aethereal impulse of the poem is turned to celestial song inspired by Urania and the music of the spheres, offering an ultimately rapturous sense of the order of creation, its ascetic one is turned to severe moral fable, requiring obedience to the commanding voice of God. Like Moses, Milton must tell of creation and he must mediate the moral law to fallen man. We may now look more fully at that moral law, at the poet justifying the ways of God to man.

The Oracle of God

It is a little ungenerous to Milton to wrest a phrase from its evocative setting and apply it to an unintended purpose:

> Or if Sion hill
> Delight thee more, and Siloa's brook that flow'd
> Fast by the oracle of God; I thence
> Invoke thy aid to my advent'rous song,

> (I, 10–13)

For within the poet's symbolic topography of Jerusalem, the 'oracle of God' is the deepest sanctuary of the Jewish temple, and the flow of Siloa's brook 'fast by' aptly expresses the relationship between the poet's song and the ultimate divine mysteries. Milton, however, compels us to think of him as the oracle of God in quite another sense—the very voice of God, His mouthpiece upon earth. He makes God speak, and dogmatically declare His nature and His grand designs. In fuller voice than Moses he would expound the laws of God, and in ampler vision than St John the Divine's he would display His cosmic purposes. Whether we marvel at Milton's courage or wonder at his cheek, we must recognise that an effort to clarify and affirm the truth about God as the Puritans conceived Him is a powerful pressure on the shaping of the poem.

While the stories of the fall of man and the fall of the angels stay where Milton first found them, in the Book of Genesis and in a few verses of Revelation (12.3–4, 7–9) and Isaiah (14.12–15), their disarming simplicity and brevity, together with their elusive mystery, allow them to stir the imagination without inviting much dogmatic or moral exposition. Their difficulties become conspicuous, however, when they are amplified, charged with specific significances, and enriched with circumstance. These processes had long been at work upon them in the various traditions of Christianity, and Milton found himself (not unwillingly) committed to theological and moral argument as well as to imaginative celebration of momentous events in a vast setting.

From one point of view the myth of the fall is among the more disconcerting of the Old Testament's insights into the nature of God. For on reflection it is hard to exempt the Creator himself from responsibility for the instabilities of Paradise—for the forbidden fruit which gives occasion for sin, for the cryptic prohibition, and for the talking serpent. The sin committed, it is profoundly punished, the punishment sustained across generations to come. Milton, however, encounters the moral instabilities of creation at an earlier stage. The fall of Satan elicited for him the perplexities that occupy the more thoughtful (and less athletic) of the delinquent angels in his hell:

> Others apart sat on a hill retir'd,
> In thoughts more elevate, and reason'd high
> Of providence, foreknowledge, will and fate,
> Fix'd fate, free will, foreknowledge absolute,
> And found no end, in wand'ring mazes lost.
>
> (II, 557–61)

How can God's goodness, omnipotence and omniscience be reconciled with the intrusion of pain and malice into his creation? To what creative ends does he allow his own purposes to be subverted? The 'false philosophy' of the fallen angels can find no answers in its wandering mazes; but Milton's God does, and Milton is his oracle in the formidable apologia offered to God the Son in Book III. Satan is observed winging his way towards 'the new created world,/ And man there plac'd',

> with purpose to assay
> If him by force he can destroy, or worse,
> By some false guile pervert; and shall pervert;
> For man will heark'n to his glozing lies,
> And easily transgress the sole command,
> Sole pledge of his obedience: so will fall
> He and his faithless progeny: whose fault?
> Whose but his own?
>
> (III, 90–7)

One may sympathise with Milton's endeavour to dramatise and humanise the divine plan while still wondering why God addresses his Son in so sardonic and irrascible a tone; for it is hard to read in a magnanimous spirit verse that so sharply features its bitterest words.

It is timely to remember, however, that the story is as important for what it says about man as about God. Milton had thought it all out many years before in *Areopagitica*—the pamphlet primarily written to win freedom of publication for his views on divorce, but growing into an acclamation of the principle of freedom in the scheme of things:

> Many there be that complain of divine Providence for suffering Adam to transgress. Foolish tongues! when God gave him reason, he gave him freedom to choose, for freedom is but choosing; he had been else a mere artificial Adam, such an Adam as he is in the motions. We ourselves esteem not of that obedience, or love, or gift, which is of force; God therefore left him free, set before him a provoking object, ever almost in his eyes; herein consisted his merit, herein the right of his reward, the praise of his abstinence.

Transposed into Milton's later verse and assigned to God, similar reflections make a different impression:

> ingrate, he had of me
> All he could have; I made him just and right,
> Sufficient to have stood, though free to fall.
> Such I created all th' ethereal powers
> And spirits, both them who stood and them who fail'd;
> Freely they stood who stood, and fell who fell.
> Not free, what proof could they have giv'n sincere
> Of true allegiance, constant faith or love,
> Where only what they needs must do, appear'd,
> Not what they would? what praise could they receive?
> What pleasure I from such obedience paid,

> When will and reason (reason also is choice)
> Useless and vain, or freedom both despoil'd,
> Made passive both, had serv'd necessity,
> Not me.
>
> (III, 97–111)

When in *Areopagitica* Milton alludes to man freely offering to God his obedience and love, the prospect is self-transcending. But when God in the poem is made to talk like a man, Milton exposes him to human judgement and he appears to be sulking because he made angels and man to serve him freely and in their freedom they chose otherwise. Is Milton's sardonic, exasperated, sulky and rigorously egocentric God a deliberate creation of the poet's art, an accidental one owed to the awkwardness of the chosen form, or an illusion shaped by the moral attitudes of readers more easy-going and cavalier than Milton? These are not easy questions to answer; nor are they the only ones.

Many have found the moral voice of the poem uncongenial, either for the harshness and insensitivity of its judgements, or for its lack of imaginative vitality. As Pope puts it:

> Milton's strong pinion now at Heaven can bound,
> Now serpent-like, in prose he sweeps the ground;
> In quibbles, angel and archangel join,
> And God the Father turns a school-divine.
>
> (*To Augustus*, 99–102)

It may be retorted that Milton's theological labours, like his moral vehemence, are capable of explanation. The dogma and even the quibbles are a part of his effort to recover for English Puritanism the 'pure' and central doctrines of the Bible, freeing them from the Calvinist impediments to human freedom ('As if predestination over-rul'd'), and from the Roman Church ('For on earth/Who against faith and conscience can be heard/Infallible?'). Hence, for instance, the answers that the poem's God supplies to the questions that troubled the angels in hell:

> They therefore as to right belong'd
> So were created, nor can justly accuse
> Their maker, or their making, or their fate;
> As if predestination over-rul'd
> Their will, dispos'd by absolute decree
> Or high foreknowledge; they themselves decreed
> Their own revolt, not I: if I foreknew,
> Foreknowledge had no influence on their fault,
> Which had no less prov'd certain unforeknown.
>
> (III, 111–19)

With such thoughts, ironically like the fallen angels, Milton might have charmed 'pain for a while' and armed 'th'obdured breast/With stubborn patience as with triple steel'; for in such questionings and answerings there is a dogged search for personal philosophic solace. But there is more than that. In his invocations to the divine muses and the Holy Spirit, Milton was striving to reach the ultimate moral truth, and through its voice to impose upon himself and upon the human race a discipline consistent with freedom.

The voice is often stern and admonitory, the 'warning voice' of the Apocalypse that cries 'Woe to th' inhabitants on earth', yet it must be consolatory and sustaining too. The sources of consolation in the poem include the confidence that patience and endurance will be ultimately vindicated, a conviction that Milton could share with the Stoics. More positively they are found in his version of the doctrine of the 'fortunate fall' (*felix culpa*) stated in its most elementary form in the assurance that Michael gives Adam, of a Second Coming when

> the earth
> Shall all be Paradise, far happier place
> Than this of Eden, and far happier days.
>
> (XII, 463–5)

and in Adam's naïve response:

> full of doubt I stand
> Whether I should repent me now of sin
> By me done and occasion'd, or rejoice
> Much more, that much more good thereof shall spring.

Confronted by the desolating account of human history unfolded
in the last books it is not easy for Adam or for Milton to keep up this
sanguine tone. It gives place to a more tragic sense of life that finds
more creative opportunities in the fallen, suffering world (Blake would
call it 'Experience') than in the unfallen state of innocence. Finally,
and most fully engaging the art of the poet, there are the consolatory
intimations of divine order offered by the splendour, symmetry and
bounty of the created planetary world.

  William Blake, the most devoted and most censorious of Milton's
admirers, believed that Milton misconceived the nature of God and
therefore could not sympathetically re-create him in poetry:

> The reason Milton wrote in fetters when he wrote of Angels &
> God, and at liberty when of Devils & Hell, is because he was a
> true Poet and of the Devil's party without knowing it.

A makeshift compromise with Blake's ideas (which have simple
beginnings but complex consequences) might claim that traditional
Christianity only imperfectly acknowledges the displacement of the
Old Testament by the New, of the cult of a jealous God—whom
Blake caricatured as 'Nobodaddy'—by the 'Everlasting Gospel' of
love and the forgiveness of sins:

> Thinking as I do that the Creator of this World is a very Cruel
> Being, & being a Worshipper of Christ, I cannot help saying:
> 'the Son, O how unlike the Father!' First God Almighty comes
> with a Thump on the Head. Then Jesus Christ comes with a
> balm to heal it.

Certainly the Old Testament holds sway over *Paradise Lost*. The
atonement of man through the incarnation and sacrifice of Christ is

only a distant prospect, and while an important theme of Milton's argument, it does not occasion a memorable poetry of 'mercy, pity, peace and love' (to name the sanctities of Blake's 'Divine Image'). On the contrary, the stress is upon the punishment that Christ will undergo on man's behalf:

> The law of God exact he shall fulfil
> Both by obedience and by love, though love
> Alone fulfil the law; thy punishment
> He shall endure by coming in the flesh
> To a reproachful life and cursed death,
> Proclaiming life to all who shall believe
> In his redemption, and that his obedience
> Imputed becomes theirs by faith, his merits
> To save them, not their own, though legal works.
> For this he shall live hated, be blasphem'd,
> Seiz'd on by force, judg'd, and to death condemn'd
> A shameful and accurs'd, nail'd to the Cross
> By his own nation, slain for bringing life.
>
> (XII, 402–14)

Thus Michael, talking as Blake would say 'in fetters', with the oracular severity characteristic of this aspect of the poem, and with grim solace: 'But to the cross he nails thy enemies.'

There is a connection between the hard enduring virtues that Milton needed to cultivate in his later years (and which he foreshadows in *Comus*) and those which he attributes to Christ in his ordeal of obedience to the will of God. For he had seen the malice that crucified Christ very much at work in contemporary England, through the judicial torturing and butchering of Puritan leaders to the cheers and shouts of hysterical London mobs. The trial and execution of Sir Henry Vane in 1662 ('By his own nation', it could be said, 'slain for bringing life') was only one of many spectacles to convince Milton that the atonement of man was a long, arduous process. *Areopagitica* was written out of a high confidence in the ability of the free people of England to build the 'goodly and graceful symmetry' of a new society; *Paradise Lost* was written not only about the fall of man but also after the fall of the commonwealth.

Neither fall, however, was irredeemable. Unlike the Levellers and the Diggers Milton paid little attention to what Aristotle called 'distributive justice', and to the economic system of the day. He attributed political evils to failures of human virtue, personal and communal. He emphatically did not believe that we are what the 'system' makes us, and would probably have treated nineteenth- and twentieth-century claims of that kind as versions of Calvinism, designed to diminish freedom and responsibility. From this point of view the myth of the fall was an admirable vehicle for his conviction, as it sets an act of intimate and personal choice at the centre of a vast cosmic and historical disturbance. And Milton finds a way of keeping the choice open; in theological language, God's grace renews man's 'lapsed powers' and enables him to stand 'On even ground against his mortal foe' (III, 179) sustained by his 'Umpire Conscience' Tasting of the forbidden fruit brings death into the world and creates the conditions under which life must be reaffirmed and re-created. 'Immortality', says Milton's God, served, once happiness was lost, 'but to eternise woe', and death is both a punishment and an act of mercy:

> so death becomes
> His final remedy, and after life
> Tri'd in sharp tribulation, and refin'd
> By faith and faithful works, to second life,
> Wak'd in the renovation of the just,
> Resigns him up with heav'n and earth renew'd.
> (XI, 61–6)

'Tri'd in sharp tribulation, and refin'd' expresses Milton's under-standing of the kind of suffering that Christ and man would undergo together. Where the Counter-Reformation set the crucifixion at the centre of religious experience, Milton set the temptation in the wilderness. In *Paradise Regained*, in some respects a sequel to *Paradise Lost*, Christ is the 'queller of Satan' who redeems the fall of Adam and Eve by exhibiting a perfect discipline of obedience. He exemplifies the constraint of passions that Milton believed would renew the moral and political life of the whole society:

> Yet he who reigns within himself, and rules
> Passions, desires, and fears, is more a king;
> Which every wise and virtuous man attains;
> And who attains not, ill aspire to rule
> Cities of men, or head-strong multitudes,
> Subject himself to anarchy within,
> Or lawless passions in him which he serves.
>   (*Paradise Regained*, II, 466–72)

Blake retorted, 'Those who restrain desire, do so because theirs is weak enough to be restrained'. In one aspect of his thought he shared Rousseau's confidence in the innocence of the child and therefore in the innocence of the human condition to which the child is born; for Rousseau thought it 'an incontrovertible rule that the first impulses of nature are always right; there is no original sin in the human heart; the how and why of the entrance of every vice can be traced'. In some moods Blake associated Milton's version of the fall with the constraints that parents in the Puritan tradition exercised over their children, as in *A Little Girl Lost*:

> To her father white
> Came the maiden bright;
> But his loving look,
> Like the holy book,
> All her tender limbs with terror shook.

But the maiden in Blake's poem offends with 'kisses sweet' and is found asleep with a youth on the grass. The fall in Milton's Eden is occasioned in no obvious way by sexual passion, but rather by the presumption that knowledge of good and evil will make man more like a god; love-making in Paradise is innocent and delightful before the fall but burning and lascivious after. But while Milton takes care of some of the difficulties in the *argument* of his poem, it is hard altogether to set aside Blake's comment on the life and quality of the verse; at crucial moments there are severe tensions between the movement of Milton's imaginative sympathies and his recognition of the astringencies of divine law; Eve, for example, speaking after Adam in 'glorious trial of exceeding love' has shared in her tasting of the fruit:

> So saying, she embrac'd him, and for joy
> Tenderly wept, much won that he his love
> Had so ennobl'd, as of choice t' incur
> Divine displeasure for her sake, or death.
> In recompense (for such compliance bad
> Such recompense best merits) from the bough
> She gave him of that fair enticing fruit
> With liberal hand: he scrupl'd not to eat
> Against his better knowledge, not deceiv'd,
> But fondly overcome with female charm.
>
> (IX, 990–9)

Milton in full and generous voice would have men free, but in the sonorous and inexorable accents that impel the opening words of the poem, 'Of man's first disobedience', he would have them do as they are told. So it is with the voices that tell of the fall—the human affections are warmly honoured, but in the parentheses and comments frigidly rebuked.

The paradoxes and mysteries relating to liberty and constraint, good and evil, have a long and continuing history, from Moses to Mao Tse-tung. Underlying the manifest differences between Milton and Blake, we find at work in both mythologies the contrary principles of energy and restraint—the one conferring life, the other form; it may be claimed that the moral experience of man has always demonstrated that there is no escaping either. Rabelais in *Gargantua and Pantagruel* (I, lii–lvii) tells in sixteenth-century France of the Abbey of Theleme where the only injunction is, 'Do what thou wilt', but he finds that perfect freedom can be allowed only to those who are perfectly virtuous. In Victorian England, the poet Arthur Hugh Clough, confronting the taboos and constraints of the day, offers another version of Milton's fortunate fall:

> What we call sin,
> I could believe a painful opening out
> Of paths for ampler virtue.
>
> (*Dipsychus*)

but Milton would have been shocked at that way of putting it.

The Starry Dance and the Fall of Man

'Discipline' is not always the most imaginatively satisfying of words, but Milton comes near to making it so in *The Reason of Church Government*:

> So that whatsoever power or sway in mortal things weaker men
> have attributed to fortune, I durst with more confidence (the
> honour of Divine Providence ever saved) ascribe either to the
> vigour or slackness of discipline. Nor is there any sociable
> perfection in this life, civil or sacred, that can be above disci-
> pline; but she is that which with her musical cords preserves
> and holds all the parts thereof together. Hence in those perfect
> armies of Cyrus in Xenophon, and Scipio in the Roman stories,
> the excellence of military skill was esteemed, not by the not
> needing, but by the readiest submitting to the edicts of their
> commander. And certainly discipline is not only the removal
> of disorder; but if any visible shape can be given to divine
> things, the very visible shape and image of virtue, whereby she
> is not only seen in the regular gestures and motions of her
> heavenly paces as she walks, but also makes the harmony of
> her voice audible to mortal ears.

Here is the principle of constraint, making social and cosmic harmony, making music.

In Milton's version of the Old Testament creation story (Book VII, 216 ff.) God takes the golden compasses and circumscribes 'this universe, and all created things', while his Spirit with 'brooding wings ... outspread' infuses the 'fluid mass' of chaos with warmth and 'vital virtue'. It is a condition of life that boundaries be imposed upon it, but they are boundaries that allow infinite scope to human wonder and delight. A solicitous astronomical order presides over the life of Paradise, discovered, for example, when Eve marvels that the stars should shine all night when 'sleep hath shut all eyes', and Adam explains:

> Daughter of God and man, accomplish'd Eve,
> Those have their course to finish, round the earth,
> By morrow ev'ning, and from land to land
> In order, though to nations yet unborn,
> Minist'ring light prepar'd, they set and rise;
> Lest total darkness should by night regain
> Her old possession, and extinguish life
> In nature and in all things, which these soft fires
> Not only enlighten, but with kindly heat
> Of various influence foment and warm,
> Temper or nourish, or in part shed down
> Their stellar virtue on all kinds that grow
> On earth, made hereby apter to receive
> Perfection from the sun's more potent ray.
>
>   (IV, 660–73)

The great diurnal harmonies of the cosmos compose the domestic rhythms of the lives of Adam and Eve. In the Paradise of Book IV there are no seasons, for the universe retains its created symmetries; but there is movement, expressed by Milton's verse—in the heavens the 'starry dance', and on earth:

> airs, vernal airs,
> Breathing the smell of field and grove, attune
> The trembling leaves, while universal Pan
> Knit with the Graces and the Hours in dance
> Led on th' eternal spring.
>
> (IV, 264–8)

Responsive to, almost obedient to the times of day, Adam and Eve enjoy their round of 'sweet gardening labour', afternoon rest, 'supper fruits' and nuptial satisfaction. Their love gives fuller significance to the ceremonious daily round; as Eve describes to Adam:

> But neither breath of morn when she ascends
> With charm of earliest birds, nor rising sun
> On this delightful land, nor herb, fruit, flow'r,
> Glist'ring with dew, nor fragrance after showers,
> Nor grateful ev'ning mild, nor silent night
> Without this her solemn bird, nor walk by moon,
> Or glitt'ring star-light without thee is sweet.
>
> (IV, 650–6)

In Book VIII Adam questions Raphael about the purposes and structure of the cosmos, wondering why the stars' motions should be centred upon the apparently negligible earth:

> When I behold this goodly frame, this world
> Of heav'n and earth consisting, and compute
> Their magnitudes, this earth a spot, a grain,
> An atom, with the firmament compar'd
> And all her number'd stars, that seem to roll
> Spaces incomprehensible (for such
> Their distance argues and their swift return
> Diurnal) merely to officiate light
> Round this opacous earth, this punctual spot,
> One day and night.
>
> (VIII, 15–24)

Raphael's reply, 'To ask or search I blame thee not', confesses the inadequacy of human and angelic understanding, and asks that man should know the 'various rounds' of the planetary dance:

> learn
> His seasons, hours, or days, or months, or years:
> This to attain, whether heav'n move or earth,
> Imports not, if thou reck'n right,
>
> (VIII, 68–71)

Raphael is content with the littleness of the earth, knowing that great or bright infers not excellence', and that the earth is fruitful where the sun is barren. Milton, through Raphael, returns us to a human centre upon this 'diurnal sphere' with its tender, poised solicitude of movement:

> Whether the sun predominant in heav'n
> Rise on the earth, or earth rise on the sun,
> He from the east his flaming road begin,
> Or she from west her silent course advance
> With inoffensive pace that spinning sleeps
> On her soft axle, while she paces ev'n,
> And bears thee soft with the smooth air along,
> Solicit not thy thoughts with matters hid,
> Leave them to God above, him serve and fear;
> Of other creatures, as him pleases best,
> Wherever plac'd, let him dispose: joy thou
> In what he gives to thee, this Paradise
> And thy fair Eve;
>
> (VIII, 160–72)

The rhythms of the stars, of human affections and of Milton's verse are intimately interrelated in passages that most fully engage the poet's art and are most fully charged with authentic religious feeling.

For a modern version of similar insights we may look to D. H. Lawrence:

Oh, what a catastrophe for man when he cut himself off from
the rhythm of the year, from his union with the sun and the
earth .... Marriage is the clue to human life, but there is no mar-
riage apart from the wheeling sun and the nodding earth, from
the straying of the planets and the magnificence of the fixed stars.
Is not a man different, utterly different, at dawn from what he
is at sunset? and a woman too? And does not the changing
harmony and discord of their variation make the secret music
of life?

Where Lawrence attributes the upsetting of the natural rhythms to
'Protestantism', however, and to the growth of a secular society,
Milton attributes it to the fall. When in Book IX the omnific word
is disobeyed, the earth tilts on its axis, the sun shifts from the equinoc-
tial, riding now from Cancer to Capricorn,

> to bring in change
> Of seasons to each clime; else had the spring
> Perpetual smil'd on earth with vernant flow'rs,
> Equal in days and nights,
>
> (X, 677–80)

'Thus began outrage from lifeless things', and creatures suffer with
creation as the earth is invaded by weather, and attendant forms of
catastrophe—fear, terror, suffering, sin, disease and death.

The diurnal rhythms remain consolatory, but more ambiguously
so. Compare, for example, the unfallen night-time of Book IV
(610–16) when 'all things now retir'd to rest/Mind us of like repose',
with the fallen one of Book X (845–52) when 'dreadful gloom'
represents to Adam's evil conscience 'All things with double terror'.
Consciousness of evil puts a blight upon the order and bounty of
creation. For the last books of the poem (particularly from the
appearance of Michael to the end of his Old Testament narrative)
the voices of praise (see, for instance the morning hymn in Book V)
are muted, and the virtue that must now be cultivated is of the classi-

cal or Stoic kind calling for fortitude, patience, moderation, temperance and self-control. The evening star, however, still rises as 'Love's harbinger' over the revellers in the tents of wickedness (XI, 588); the sun dries up the deluge, and the rainbow promises that

> day and night,
> Seed time and harvest, heat and hoary frost
> Shall hold their course, till fire purge all things new,
> Both heav'n and earth, wherein the just shall dwell.
> (XI, 898–901)

The seasons, once a tempered punishment, have become our principa solace.

Books One and Two

The fall of Satan begins in Hebrew and Christian mythology as an event in the morning and evening sky. The planet Venus (the morning star, Lucifer) which can still surprise us by its brilliance in the east before it is outshone by the sun, and in the west before it falls below the horizon, was taken by the prophet Isaiah as a symbol for the arrogance and decline of the King of Babylon:

Hell from beneath is moved for thee to meet thee at thy coming: it stirreth up the dead for thee, even all the chief ones of the earth; it hath raised up from their thrones all the kings of the nations. All they shall speak and say unto thee, Art thou also become weak as we? art thou become like unto us? Thy pomp is brought down to the grave, and the noise of thy viols: the worm is spread under thee, and the worms cover thee. How art thou fallen from heaven, O Lucifer, son of the morning? how art thou cut down to the ground, which didst weaken the nations! For thou hast said in thine heart, I will ascend into heaven, I will exalt my throne above the stars of God: I will sit also upon the mount of the congregation, in the sides of the north: I will ascend above the heights of the clouds; I will be like the Most High. Yet thou shalt be brought down to hell, to the sides of the pit. They that seek thee shall narrowly look upon thee, and consider thee, saying, Is this the man that made the earth to tremble, that did shake kingdoms; that made the world as a wilderness, and destroyed the cities thereof?

(Isaiah 14. 9–17)

There, in little, is the celestial perspective of *Paradise Lost*, some of its moral and political force, and an aspect of its plot.

The stars, the climb above the clouds, give scale to the moral offence while at the same time recalling us to the littleness and finitude of man. When Marlowe's Faustus asks of Mephistophiles how he fell to become the prince of devils, he is answered, 'O, by aspiring pride and insolence,/For which God threw him from the face of heaven'. The fallen angels of Hebrew story, like the fallen deities and sub-deities of the Greeks, exemplify the moral risk to which the highest forms of aspiration are exposed. In many theologies and mythologies 'pride' or 'hubris' (as the Greeks called it) is the source of most, if not all, of the possible crimes and vices. But in this sense it must be defined with greater amplitude than we are accustomed to in the range of meanings which bring 'pride' close to 'vanity'; it comprehends the ultimate presumptions by which man mistakes his limited life for the whole of life, his limited power for omnipotence; these are the presumptions that prompt man to set himself above the law, and therefore to sin. Milton makes the traditional points in astringent phrases ('obdurate pride and stead-fast hate', 'fix'd mind and high disdain', 'from sense of injur'd merit'), but his version is most impressive where it enlists a spacious cosmic setting, with sensations of vertigo and void. The ruined light of the evening sky, and the falling light of meteors and setting stars, are the dominant metaphors of moral decline, and it is apt that the action begins with Lucifer's catastrophic flight through space (I, 44–9).

Movement, syntax and metaphor create in the poem a symbolic pageantry that owes much to the changing moods of the elements (sunrise and sunset, noon stillness, storm and darkness) and to cosmic events. When Satan, for example, reviews his assembling armies (I, 589–601) the strange shape which stands 'like a tow'r', bright in form, commanding in gesture, but 'ruin'd' and 'obscur'd', is readily present to an imagination familiar with cloudscapes. It gives way perfectly naturally to the dawn's 'horizontal misty air', the thunder-scars and the eclipse. The romantic painter John Martin responded well to this aspect of the poem, making from the sky and the sea an imaginary territory of space and fire; while in our own time the great Russian film-producer Eisenstein has admired Milton's changing spatial imagery and has found equivalents for it in the *montage* of his own cinema.[1]

The subtler celestial motions, as well as the sky's pageantry, are transposed into Milton's poetry. The moon's motion, for instance, presides over the 'faery elves' that,

> some belated peasant sees,
> Or dreams he sees, while overhead the moon
> Sits arbitress, and nearer to the earth
> Wheels her pale course,
>
> (I, 783–6)

Milton's imagination, more comprehensive than the peasant's, uses the course of the moon in the broken light of the evening sky to express Satan's motion over the lake of fire:

> He scarce had ceas'd when the superior fiend
> Was moving toward the shore; his ponderous shield
> Ethereal temper, massy, large and round,

[1] Sergei Eisenstein, *The Film Sense*, trans. J. Leyda (1943) pp. 52–7

> Behind him cast; the broad circumference
> Hung on his shoulders like the moon, whose orb
> Through optic glass the Tuscan artist views
> At ev'ning from the top of Fesole,
> Or in Valdarno, to descry new lands,
> Rivers or mountains in her spotty globe.
>
> (I, 283–91)

The marvel is that such weight and mass should move with the rhythmic ease that Milton's verse insinuates. In part it is accomplished by control of caesura (the medial pauses within the lines) and metric pace—the trochaic pulse of line 285, for example, and the poised weighting of 'Hung', 'moon' and 'orb' in line 287; but in part by the changing perspective of reverie—the moon recalled by a memory of Homer's shield of Achilles, enlarged by the miraculous optic glass of Galileo, and Galileo himself diminished by the breadth and wondering remoteness of the poet's vision. The poetry is simple in its large effects, subtle in its finer evocations. The awe we are made to feel for the 'Tuscan artist' Galileo, for example, is called out from the spell of names—*Fesole* and *Valdarno*, but the spell is cast too by Milton's delight in knowledge and discovery. In this voice Milton speaks as heir to Marlowe, participating in intellectual adventure and enjoying the resonance of the places of the earth in a confidently spacious rhythm. The aspiration of Galileo is endorsed in the processes of a poetry which is re-creating the aspiration and fall of Satan.

The Deep Tract of Hell

Most accounts of hell current in Milton's time were preoccupied with its function as a place of punishment for the souls of the damned; they sometimes raised awkward questions—were all tormented alike or were there degrees of ordeal? what became of unbaptized children and of those who died in ignorance of the Christian faith? were there more souls in hell than in heaven? and (most important) was God's justice therapeutic or merely vindictive? Most of these questions, and many related ones had been entertained by Dante, for whom the progress of the soul after death is very variously and subtly adjusted to the quality of the life on earth. It is the more remarkable then, that with such precedents in the theology and poetry of hell, Milton's hell is scarcely a human destination at all and no questions are raised about its modes of punitive justice. We learn from Book X that a prodigious bridge is built over chaos 'To make the way easier from hell to this world to and fro', but its memorable function is to facilitate the invasion of the earth by the forces of evil:

> See with what heat these dogs of hell advance
> To waste and havoc yonder world, which I
> So fair and good created,
>
> (X, 616–18)

Hell in *Paradise Lost* is pre-eminently the source of evil energies contaminating and complicating human life on earth. The vindictive punishment of God—the infliction of eternal torment to no saving purpose—is manifestly the destiny of the fallen angels. For fallen man, Milton re-states the judgements of the God of Genesis:

> In the sweat of thy face shalt thou eat bread,
> Till thou return unto the ground, for thou
> Out of the ground was taken, know thy birth,
> For dust thou art, and shalt to dust return.
>
> (X, 205–8)

Milton's significant amplification of his text is the ironic injunction, 'know thy birth', for within this knowledge (acquired from the forbidden fruit) is the whole human discovery of mortality as foreseen by Michael in the last books—childbirth, work, disease, old age and death, within the cycle of dust. But the mortal state is redeemable, and the earth that is given to man 'to possess and rule' is 'no despicable gift' (XI, 340), but susceptible still to the 'waste and havoc' that have their springs in hell.

It does not follow, however, that because hell is primarily the destined state of fallen angels and not of fallen man, it therefore lacks a human content and significance. When Satan falls to 'bottom-less perdition' his state conjoins a spatial, sensational horror—the notion of an absolute abyss, with moral horror—a condition of total deprivation from joy and solace. The physical and moral worlds are intimately related in human experience through the imagination, in waking musings, in dream and in hallucination; and poets have always exploited the relationship. Milton's contemporary, Sir Thomas Browne, nicely expressed what many have felt when he mocked the 'flaming mountains, which to grosser apprehensions represent hell', and confessed, 'I feel sometimes a hell within myself; Lucifer keeps his court in my breast, legion is revived in me'. But this way of putting it fails to recognise that the 'flaming mountains' can be the imagery of the hell within, expressions of the tormented consciousness.

The imagery of hell available to Milton had sources in poetic traditions both Hebrew and classical. In England much had been absorbed into drama, both in direct form (as in Marlowe's *Dr Faustus*) and obliquely, as in Kyd's *Spanish Tragedy* and several of the tragedies of Shakespeare. In the *Spanish Tragedy* the ghost tells of 'Pluto's court' and within it the 'left-hand path' that leads to 'the deepest hell,/Where bloody Furies shake their whips of steel'. Such is the spectacle of hell; but later in the play the distracted avenger speaks of 'a path upon your left-hand side, /That leadeth from a guilty conscience/Unto a forest of distrust and fear,/A darksome place, and dangerous to pass'. Thus conscience (or consciousness) creates in the imagination the landscapes and instruments of pain, states and punish-ments for offences against moral convictions.

The Bible's versions of hell, the apocryphal versions and the classi-cal underworld are stylised and public renderings of territories that are phantasmagoric and fragmentary in the intimate moral experience of individuals. Thus the vision of Shakespeare's King Lear when he awakens to tears of remorse from his trance at Dover:

> I am bound
> Upon a wheel of fire, that mine own tears
> Do scald like molten lead.

is an intimate re-creation of an idea found in the *Apocalypse of Peter*: 'the untiring river of fire shall flow . . . out of the great river shall a wheel of fire encompass them, because they devised wicked works'. Similarly, Shakespeare makes the desolating phantasmagoric and hallucinatory ordeal of Macbeth out of the traditional imagery of darkness ('hell is murky') and out of fragmentary recollections of the Bible (compare 'Pity like a naked new-born babe' with the blast of God's avenging breath in Psalm 18).

   Milton's hell, like Virgil's underworld, is less inward, less personal than those glimpsed from Shakespeare, but it is close both to the cosmic spectacles of the Book of Revelation and to the subterranean and volcanic regions of the earth. The created world itself offers rivers and lakes of fire, dark seas and capacious dungeons, reminding us that the 'fire and brimstone' of biblical terror are actual as well as metaphoric. Hence the mining of sulphur and 'ribs of gold' under a belching volcano (I, 670 ff.) is an exotic earthly event as well as a hellish; the potentials of hell are co-extensive with the more obscure and more lurid potentials of the world we know. But the actual is allegorised too. It may be true, as one scholar has suggested, that Milton's hell is a transfigured memory of the Phlegrean Fields outside Naples where, according to one seventeenth-century account, the soil 'sounds and rattles like a drum . . . and you may feel boiling waters under your feet', and where 'You would think yourself almost in the midst of hell; where all things appear horrid, sad and lamentable, with a most formidable face of things'. In *Paradise Lost* the 'formidable face of things' gives magnitude and intensity to spiritual distress. Within the immense twenty-five line sentence (I, 50-74) which opens the account of hell, multiplying clauses disclose expanding and interminable prospects of pain and deprivation. Here, the phrase 'darkness visible' has the paradoxical density associated with the more meditative poetry of Milton's time, disturbing both intellect and senses; while 'hope never comes that comes to all' is the sort of comprehensive moral aphorism to be found in Dante, but inescapably related to continuing physical torment. Suffering that is ambiguously mental and physical ('affliction and dismay') is transposed into fiery landscape, with the tortures alike of vast space ('waste and wild') and cruel confinement.

To our 'grosser apprehensions', to borrow Thomas Browne's phrase, the flaming mountains and burning marl of the 'deep tract of hell' may do more to excite the imagination than to touch the moral understanding. They belong to the cult of the spectacular sublime, with which Milton was familiar in the art and theatre of contemporary Italy. They witness to abilities in Milton that would be recognised by John Martin, by Edmund Burke and by Dr Johnson, 'the power of displaying the vast, illuminating the splendid, enforcing the awful, darkening the gloomy, and aggravating the dreadful'. Spectacle can be subdued to moral purpose, and the sensational ordeals by fire are in part intended to satisfy the spectators' appetites for vindictive punishment (see the story of Dives and Lazarus in Luke 16). In *Paradise Lost* the excitements of spectacle are assimilated into a larger experience. For the fall does not exhaust the creative resources of the angels in the abyss; out of the raw materials of fire, pain and despair, they re-assemble an epic army, build a vast city, and hold a council of war.

'Resolution from Despair'

The range of allusion and the sonority of Milton's poetic dialect, so well fitted to express the spacious reverberating miseries of the abyss, serve also to convince us of the possibilities of recovery. Satan's cry, 'What though the field be lost?/All is not lost', strikes a note that must often have been heard after the actual as well as the mythical battles of the pagan and Christian worlds; and Beëlzebub's response, 'the mind and spirit remains/Invincible, and vigour soon returns', is as apt for courage in human defeat as in angelic fall. Milton's imaginative sympathies are fully engaged in the act of re-creating the spirit of heroic resistance, and his verse confers an ample epic resonance upon Satan's marshalling of the energies of evil throughout Books I and II.

The cumulative, proliferating effects characteristic of Milton's syntax and metaphor, are a principal source of the narrative progress too; the desolations of hell grow more populous, various and active as the poem advances under an impetus that we may call either Satanic (commending the devils' resourcefulness) or Miltonic (commending the poet's). The figure of Satan is given an expanding presence and significance in the dimensions of dream, legend, and ancient and Biblical history. When he speaks 'with head uplift above the wave', he is like the giants of Greek legend who rebelled against Zeus in the classical version of the war in heaven (I, 198), but also like the 'sea-beast/Leviathan' of the Psalms, and therefore a whale for the marvelling seamen to tell stories about. He is at once unreal and actual, and will not stay to be questioned—for the Greek names allude to several figures, episodes and places which are imperfectly related in Milton's narrative (see note on I, 197–208); the whale turns into a sea-serpent, alluding perhaps to the 'crooked serpent' of Isaiah, but into the 'scaly rind' of this symbolic beast the 'night-founder'd skiff', can lodge its anchor. The phrase 'night-founder'd' would startle if it were simply an element in the seamen's tall story, as 'foundered' means 'plunged to the bottom'. But the kind of attention required of us allows us to tolerate an imprecise sense like 'benighted' or 'overwhelmed by night', while the imagination obscurely recognises the genesis of Satan from darkness, fear and vulnerability, while the 'wished morn delays'.

The familiar but mysterious created world is transmuted into dream territory, phantasmagoria, as the slumbering whale is displaced by the uprearing serpent and the wings of a great bird—the ordinary miracle of flight made more awesome by the burden of the word 'incumbent' which 'aloft' and 'air' are made to carry: 'Aloft, incumbent on the dusky air' (I, 226). Satan strides across a volcanic terrain

made from the 'combustible/And fuell'd entrails' of Aetna. There is a
touch of indignity—like a cat on hot bricks—which Milton acknow-
ledges ('such resting found the sole/Of unblest feet'), but the recovery
of poise and power remains impressive:

> Nath'less he so endur'd, till on the beach
> Of that inflamed sea, he stood and call'd
> His legions, angel forms, who lay entranc'd
> Thick as autumnal leaves that strow the brooks
> In Vallombrosa, where th' Etrurian shades
> High overarch'd imbow'r;
>
> (I, 299–304)

The traditional element in the epic simile confers the proper teeming
magnitude—the multitudinous ghosts of Virgil's Hades (*Aeneid*,
VI, 310)—but the leaves falling upon the water are the debris of a
sheltered and privileged summer landscape, and the crowded
syllables of 'Vallombrosa' and 'Etrurian' participate in the sonorities
of ruin before recalling us to the woods outside Florence (see note
on I, 302–4). The simile is sustained past the sedge floating on the
Red Sea, from the thickly strewn debris of a pastoral paradise to the
debris of war—the 'floating carcasses/And broken chariot wheels'
of the hosts of Busiris (see note on lines 304–13). Again, Milton's
magniloquence is essential to the effect. Who but Milton would
have called the Israelites 'The sojourners of Goshen'? But the phrase
makes the familiar event remote, and freshly to be wondered at.

The 'various names,/And various idols through the heathen world'
make up the prolific procession of two hundred and fifty lines at the
centre of Book I. Hell here is most conspicuously the source of the
world's evils, many of which are attributed in prospect to the worship
of false gods. The exuberance of the scene is very much in the heroic
strain—'Ten thousand banners rise into the air/With orient colours
waving'. The deities and sanctities of territories outside Christendom
invade and contaminate the immense verbal world that Milton

fashions from place names. Although defeated, the triumphs of this host are still to come, and they represent a formidable threat to the mediterranean dominions of the true God (e.g. I, 402). Milton needs little else for his purpose but the basic material of biblical and classical history, but the allusions are intricate (as the notes testify) and the spell of words finely woven. The renewed invocation to the Muse, based on precedents in Homer and Virgil (see note on I, 376) is cast in a manner that anticipates Yeats's rendering of the arrogance and violence of Byzantium:

> Say, Muse, their names then known, who first, who last,
> Rous'd from their slumber, on that fiery couch,
> At their great emperor's call . . .

> (I, 376–8)

But Milton appears to have a Turkish rather than a Byzantine figure in mind at other moments of the poem (see I, 348, and note), and alongside the hostility of Israelites to Ammonites, Philistines and Egyptians he insinuates the crusading antagonisms of Western Christendom to the Saracens (I, 582–7). Heroic conflict seems to become a cosmic and terrestrial necessity, with pathos and music attending upon the menace and the cruelty. The Syrian rites of Thammuz exemplify the pathos (see I, 446–52, and note), with more distant effects in the Sidonian Virgins singing to the bright image of Astoreth 'whom the Phoenicians call'd/Astarte, queen of heav'n, with crescent horns' (see I, 437–41); the first is the pathos of pain, the second the pathos of human aspiration, prompted by the moon's beauty but strangely betrayed by it. As in the Nativity Ode, Milton's aesthetic sympathies with the pagan sanctities are deeply stirred, but the more militant Christian and Puritan range of his convictions move him to dismissive contempt and even violence. The Ode's day of judgement (the 'horrid clang', 'red fire' and 'smouldering clouds' of Stanza XVII) will drive Apollo from his shrine, 'With hollow shriek the steep of Delphos leaving'. *Paradise Lost* disposes of the 'Ionian gods' with another mode of pathos, allowing the flight of

Saturn 'over Adria to th' Hesperian fields' (I, 520) to establish the
valedictory tone. But the Greek heroic spirit is very potent in the
assembled angelic march, led by Azazel, whose imperial ensign
'Shone like a meteor streaming to the wind', with 'all the while
/Sonorous metal blowing martial sounds'. The 'shout that tore
hell's concave' (I, 542) is not merely an incongruous noise, but the
triumphant response to Satan's call, and a sign of liberation; the
onward movement of the angels has the disciplined harmony that
Milton admired in times of peace and war (see above p. 42), and it is
aptly commemorated in his verse:

> anon they move
> In perfect phalanx to the Dorian mood
> Of flutes and soft recorders; such as rais'd
> To highth of noblest temper heroes old
> Arming to battle, and instead of rage
> Deliberate valour breath'd, firm and unmov'd
>
> (I, 549–54)

The attribution of heroic virtue to the powers of evil has complex
consequences for the scheme of the poem.

When Satan and Beëlzebub glory 'as gods' in 'their own recover'd
strength' Milton reminds us that they owed it to 'the sufferance of
supernal power' (I, 241), not to their own invincible attributes. It
was important that Milton should from time to time remind us, and
remind himself, that God and Satan, good and evil, are not, by ortho-
dox Christian belief, co-eternal and matched in power. Manichean
doctrines, claiming that the sovereignty of the universe is perpetu-
ally contested by the rival princes of light and darkness, were found
heretical by most Christian churches, because they challenged the
omnipotence, of God and allowed too much presence and dignity to
evil. In the large order of *Paradise Lost* Milton's account of the devil
is orthodox enough; for when Satan in Book X returns in triumph
from Eden, his acclamations are met, not with the expected 'high
applause' but with 'A dismal universal hiss, the sound/Of public

scorn'. This humiliating political situation is an appropriate interpretation of the Genesis story of the serpent-tempter made to go on his belly in the dust.

In the first books of the poem, however, 'the sound of public scorn' can have no place—the devils rising from the burning lake honour Satan as their leader and 'emperor', and they are 'godlike shapes and forms excelling human'. We shall learn in Book X that 'some say' that they were turned into serpents and made to undergo an 'annual humbling certain number'd days,/To dash their pride' (X, 575-7). Milton thus humbles his devils at intervals in the opening pages (I, 126, 214-15, 240-1, 341, 361-2) but not without embarrassment, as in the disclaimer when the climactic moment of the procession approaches:

> but he his wonted pride
> Soon recollecting, with high words, that bore
> Semblance of worth, not substance, gently rais'd
> Their fainting courage, and dispell'd their fears.
> (I, 527-30)

Milton does not create the difficulty, however, he inherits it, from literary tradition and from the history of the race. 'Virtue', the poem reminds us, has an heroic sense as well as a moral, and the two are tantalisingly related. Thus Satan mocks his angels for choosing hell 'After the toil of battle to repose/Your wearied virtue' (I, 320), and when in Book II the poets among the angels 'sing/With notes angelical to many a harp/Their own heroic deeds and hapless fall/By doom of battle' (II, 547-50), they complain that 'fate/Free virtue should enthral to force or chance'. In an heroic society based on war it is hard to disengage *virtus* (to use the Latin form) meaning 'manliness' or 'valour', from more comprehensive and humane forms of goodness. For a good part of *Paradise Lost*, particularly in Books, I, II, V and VI (the war in heaven), the fallen angels compose such a society, and their impressiveness accords with its values. Isaiah had recognised that evil, made mean and contemptible after the fall in Eden, renewed its transient power and glory in the empire of Babylon, and he invokes the same laws of pride and fall to destroy it.

Pandemonium

The survey of false gods and their cults claims implicitly that the heroic virtues can co-exist with execrable vices—human sacrifice, lustful orgies, wanton rites, dark idolatries, and monstrous shapes and sorceries. In phrases less hyperbolic than Milton's we are made to recognise that efficiency and courage in war (even in defeat) are compatible with many kinds of barbarism, inhumanity and insensitivity. But among the more pernicious false sanctities is Belial (I, 490–505). He represents, not a formal cult, but the permissive spirit that reigns in 'courts' and 'in luxurious cities, where the noise/Of riot ascends above their loftiest tow'rs,/And injury and outrage'. At this moment of the poem the analogy between the Old Testament prophets' indictments of the city cultures of the Middle East, and the Puritan hostility to Restoration London is particularly sharp; but in the building of Pandemonium it is consummated and amplified, to take in ancient Babylon and Cairo (I, 717–18) and, some would say, Renaissance Rome. Milton gives the devil his due, for the proud engineering, architectural and decorative skills that fashion the city of the damned out of fire and music are not undervalued (I, 692–717). It may be doubted that Milton intended initiate readers to identify Pandemonium with St Peter's and the Vatican (noticing, for example, that bees—theme of the simile in lines 767 to 777—were the emblems of Pope Urban VIII, who dedicated St Peter's) for the architectural details would serve for many real and imagined structures in the classical traditions. But the Satanic 'virtue' is certainly capable of a superb and magnificent city fabric very remote from the values celebrated in Milton's pastoral paradise.

The architect of Pandemonium is Mulciber whose 'hand was known/In heav'n by many a tow'red structure high' (I, 732–33). His fall is a poignant expression of Milton's equivocal relationship with the classical past:

> Nor was his name unheard or unador'd
> In ancient Greece; and in Ausonian land
> Men call'd him Mulciber; and how he fell
> From heav'n, they fabl'd, thrown by angry Jove
> Sheer o'er the crystal battlements: from morn
> To noon he fell, from noon to dewy eve,
> A summer's day; and with the setting sun
> Dropp'd from the zenith like a falling star,
> On Lemnos th' Aegean isle: thus they relate,
> Erring; for he with his rebellious rout
> Fell long before. . .
>
> (I, 738–48)

The leisured fall through serene, luminous space, its excitement and its pathos, are of Milton's generous re-creating. The rigorous disclaimer at the end does not diminish it, and one feels that the rejection of the pagan world and its values is made with great effort.

It is not, in the end, a rejection but a complex process of assimilation. Milton's heaven as well as his hell has its pagan attributes; the many cities of the world represented in Pandemonium are fallen versions of Mulciber's city of the 'empyreal heav'n' glimpsed at the end of Book II (1049–50) and approached by its gateway in Book III (501–15). The opulence of heaven, with its opal towers, battlements of living sapphire and portal 'thick with sparkling orient gems', should satisfy the taste of the proudest king of Babylon.

The Great Consult

The splendours and excitements attendant upon power are allowed to the luxuriously imperial figure of Satan at the start of the second book, but Milton proclaims them with moral severity and admiring venom. Satan's 'merit' is real but hubristic, focusing at once Milton's regard for charismatic leadership and his humane resentment of the presumption of tyrants. The accretions of 'barbaric pearl and gold' cast him as an Asiatic despot, but the opulence (as we have seen) is not inconsistent with heavenly and indeed biblical taste.

The council over which Satan presides is a visionary allegory of a complex but recurring political situation, one in which the defeated look for the spirit and the tactics with which to confront an invincible enemy. It is allegory and not drama because there is no obligation upon the poet to make his figures into 'characters', to confer upon them a diversity of human attributes and idiosyncrasies. They express rival impulses of the human consciousness, however, and therefore the conflicting attitudes that are apt to be represented in council and debate; and it is worth remembering that in the course of debate a man may, as it were, allegorise himself, intensifying a single conviction, embodying a single drive. Thus the council scene is convincing both as a moral spectacle in the tradition of Spenser and as an episode in political government.

The procedures are properly democratic, with all points of view given a formal hearing under the chairmanship of an elected and acclaimed leader. But the leadership holds subtle sway over the course of the argument and over the cumulative responses of enthusiasm and dismay. Satan states his own role and position with authoritative economy while declaring the dominant motive and assumptions of debate. His version of the doctrine of the fortunate fall (see p. 36) carries a burden of equivocal truth:

> From this descent
> Celestial virtues rising, will appear
> More glorious and more dread than from no fall,
>
> (II, 14–16)

Satan's creed, 'Evil be thou my good', and his conviction that 'The mind is its own place, and in itself/Can make a heav'n of hell, a hell of heav'n' (I, 254–55), work with sophisticating wit upon the language of received morality. He offers the assurances of 'immortal vigour' and diabolical solidarity ('union, and firm faith') which seem to need no sanction outside themselves, offered as they are in casual confidence of tone. In another cogent equivocal truth, egalitarian solidarity is represented as a prerogative of hell, because all are equal in a society in which there is 'no good/For which to strive' (II, 30–31); it is not a falsehood but a sharp insight into some modes of egalitarian community, yet it is a maimed truth, for on reflection we know that there can be unity in evil causes, and faction can be prompted by ugly ambitions very remote from the hubristic aspirations that Satan characterises as 'striving for good'.

Moloch, the 'horrid king besmear'd with blood' of Book I (392–405), is here the nihilistic advocate of war. Comparisons made with Shakespeare's Hotspur are not inept (although they are a ready way of demonstrating that Milton's method is not dramatic) and may remind us that Moloch represents one of the inescapable presences in the spirit of resistance. Without some readiness to turn violence into aspiration and some element of desperate defiance, rebellions are unlikely to prosper, whether in the cosmos, or in Hotspur's, or in Cromwell's England. The brutal simplicities of Moloch's disposition express profound human propensities and obsessions which can be very fully engaged in the moral system that Milton takes over from the traditional myth; for Moloch's commitment to vindictive vengeance is a precise reaction against the vindictive punishment apparently inflicted by the God of the myth. Aspiration is transposed into violence at Moloch's prospect of the angels climbing out of ruin ('in our proper motion we ascend') in order to turn tortures back upon the torturer, and it grows nihilistic where it accepts the possibility that the angelic essence ('essential') will be reduced to nothing. The consolations of Pandemonium have no reality for Moloch. Milton allows the penal fire and the infernal city, the misery and the magnificence, to co-exist throughout the process of the debate, the presence of each diminishing or advancing according to the dominant strain of the discourse.

'Belial, in act more graceful and humane' is (as the word 'humane' here signifies) civilised and sophisticated. His 'persuasive accent' is

cogently simulated in cool, level speech rhythms that invite a slight
drawl (II, 119–23); and his opening manoeuvres are adroit, moving
promptly from eagerness to concur, by way of a compliment (Moloch
'most excels in fact of arms') to total repudiation. Belial dismisses the
nihilism of Moloch by appeal to his own vindictive principle—the
'almighty victor' (Moloch's 'torturer') will not allow the privilege of
oblivion to the heroic suicide but 'save to punish endless'. He recog-
nises the omnipotence of the Almighty (II, 170–86), his omni-
science (II, 188–90) and even his justice (II, 199–201); and his argu-
ment is sustained from central human experiences and convictions.
Hence the resonant tragic questioning of the nihilistic impulse is very
much from a human centre: 'for who would lose/Though full of
pain, this intellectual being,/Those thoughts that wander through
eternity . . .?' A comparison with Claudio's plea for life in *Measure
for Measure* (III.i.119–133: 'Ay, but to die, and go we know not
where . . .') would again measure Milton's distance from intimately
felt human drama; but in the grand dialect of the council chamber of
Pandemonium the question strikes a poignant and resonant note,
for it is Milton's as well as Belial's. A related human insight prompts
the lines about habituation to suffering (one may think, as often,
about Milton's blindness): 'Our purer essence . . . will receive/Familiar
the fierce heat, and void of pain;/This horror will grow mild, this
darkness light'. Although Belial, offering the solace of partial recovery
and inurement, seems remote from his votaries in Book I, 'flown with
insolence and wine', both his wisdom and their 'outrage' may be
attributed to the culture of 'courts and palaces' which Milton is
repudiating. Milton's immediate gloss on Belial's speech, however,
seems gratuitously to devalue it (II, 226–8); it is not to be easily
set aside.

It is not set aside in Mammon's contribution, but rather amplified
and intensified, with a new creative dimension. Mammon's com-
manding mastery of the economy of debate (229–237) confers a kind
of intellectual authority on his bitter but disconcertingly precise
characterisation of the role of the angels in Milton's heaven (239–

49). A subtle, keen control of phrases insinuates a greater mystery and energy into the state of 'hard liberty' won from 'splendid vassalage'; the 'void of pain' becomes the 'vast recess' in which the spirit moves 'Free, and to none accountable'. The metaphor from thunder-clouds (264–70) and the allusion to the 'desert soil' with its 'gems and gold' re-creates the terrestial analogy with hell, and brings Mammon's proposals for the creation of wealth through work very close to human endeavour after the fall, bringing 'ease out of pain /Through labour and endurance'. The 'magnificence' of hell (and therefore of its earthly equivalents) is hard-won through the exercise of arduous determination, and the cogency of Mammon's dialectic is a verbal manifestation of that determination—one who can so speak, must so prevail; hence our readiness to acquiesce in his spaciously reassuring conclusion (II, 278–83).

The simile describing the murmuring applause of the assembly returns us to a human situation in the natural world, making the experience of hell touch more intimately our sympathies and our senses (II, 284–90). Taught partly by Virgil, who had compared the gods' applause of Juno to the ominous wind that stirs the forest before a storm (*Aeneid* X, 96–9), Milton evokes the phenomena, the sounds and rhythms of the sea, to render human ordeal, exhaustion and solace in an elemental setting. The solace is a memory and consequence of the ordeal, 'as when hollow rocks retain/The sound of blust'ring winds, which all night long/Had rous'd the sea'; survival is fortuitous ('by chance') and in a 'craggy bay', but the 'sea-faring men' are 'o'erwatch'd', testifying to sustained effort. The effects of the metaphor, however, are severely qualified by Milton's diminishing strictures on the devils' 'fear of thunder', their 'policy' and 'emulation'.

The intervention of Beëlzebub contributes more promptly to the spectacle than to the argument; the inert metaphor, 'A pillar of state', takes life from moral attributes ('deliberation', 'public care') related to monumental ones ('front engrav'n', 'Majestic though in ruin'), to a memory of Atlas, and to qualities of atmosphere ('atten-

tion still as night/Or summer's noon-tide air'). It is Milton's evoca-
tion of what Aristotle called *ethos* in rhetoric (as distinct from its
logos and *pathos*, its argument and feeling); Beëlzebub's vast and
luminous *presence* is as commanding as his exposition. His proposals
encompass and overreach those which have won 'the popular vote';
they recognise the sovereignty of the 'king of heaven' over hell,
prohibiting projects of both peace and war, but finding scope in an
'easier enterprise' for many forms of angelic malice—vengeance,
emulation, violent and subtle destruction. The analogy between
earth and hell seems to recede as they are set at a distance from one
another in the cosmos, and the 'new race call'd Man' is apparently
menaced by non-human adversaries, not by his own propensities.
But there is still ample evidence of Milton's power 'earth with hell/
To mingle and involve'; the earth, precariously placed in the topo-
graphy of space, is like the border-territory of a kingdom, 'left/To their
defence who hold it', and the choice of strategies of destruction offered
by Beëlzebub (II, 360–70) is commonplace in the history of war.

The movement of the whole debate, as Milton reminds us, has
been towards the vindication of Satan's first malignant designs against
the new creation (I, 650–4; II, 379–85). The pathos of its imminent
invasion ('faded bliss/Faded so soon') and the proud, exulting
resolution that the prospect of it stimulates ('joy/Sparkl'd in all their
eyes; with full assent/They vote') are only slightly tempered by
Milton's intervention to save the divine plan—'their spite still
serves/His glory to augment'. The irony of Milton's rendering of the
political situation, however, is potent enough: the democratic
process has triumphantly and unanimously acclaimed the meanest
and most spiteful of all the impulses of rebellion.

That impulse, however, it to acquire its own heroic form: an
immense task, and a hero to accomplish it. Milton's poetic art is
again devoted to the re-creation of zones of air, light and darkness,
and to effects of flight and fall (II, 393–410). Satan's commendation
of the assembly ('synod of gods') transposes its virulent intentions
into aspiration; the consolations and securities of heaven are recalled

in wistful, tender phrases and cadences; the demand, 'whom shall we send/In search of this new world', is nostalgic and adventurous before it is sinister; and the prospect of the journey is of an Odyssey, a perilous return home to the regions of heaven, to the solace of 'the happy isle'. The challenge at this point is of evils to overcome, not of evils to be generated. Significantly, perhaps, Milton in his blindness recalls 'the darkness which may be felt' sent by God to plague the Egyptians (Exodus 10.21), finds the articulatory phrase, 'palpable obscure', to express it (making the lips touch the void), and enlists our imaginative sympathies for the traveller who must move through it. He evokes the terrible, vulnerable uncertainty of the blind (II, 404-6) and the heroic efforts of will ('indefatigable wings') required to master it; but the scale is astronomical, requiring the full resonance and remoteness of Milton's language—the 'uncouth way' and the 'vast abrupt'.

Satan's challenge, the muted response to it, and his own spectacular declaration 'this enterprise/None shall partake with me', are all part of the theatre of leadership. Milton's political discoveries in Pandemonium have to do both with democratic relationships—debates, elections, mass feelings, responses to leadership, and monarchical ones—the skills, responsibilities and commitments of a sovereign figure. Satan, by Milton's account, is properly 'Conscious of highest worth', and in this episode his heroic 'virtue' is extended into civic virtue. In matters of 'public moment' Satan as monarch is ready 'to accept as great a share/Of hazard as of honour, due alike/To him who reigns'. 'for the general safety he despis'd/His own', says Milton, endorsing the commendation of the fallen angels, 'for neither do the spirits damn'd/Lose all their virtue'. We may be left to wonder whether this last aside, and the lines that follow (483-5) are ingenuous or ironic. Milton himself may have felt uneasy about the inescapable parallel we discover in the poem between Satan's undertaking the journey to earth for man's destruction, and the Son undertaking it for his salvation (Book III, 217 ff.). The episode in Book II is incomparably finer, for the responses of the Son and the

angels to God's demand for 'rigid satisfaction, death for death'
(III, 212) are determined by doctrine; the muteness of the 'heavenly
choir' is an embarrassment, and the Son does not need to overcome
apprehensions and space hazards as Satan does. Milton, it may be
thought, intervenes to devalue Satan's self-effacing virtue by making
him quick to forestall emergent rivals (II, 466–73), but the point is
well made out of an insight into the tactics of human politics; the
simplicities of leadership are established, and this is the terror of the
outcome as well as its triumph—'Towards him they bend/With
awful reverence prone; and as a god/Extol him equal to the highest
in heav'n'.

The auspicious harmonies of the evening sky after a squall (II,
488–95) endorse the 'concord' of hell, leaving Milton to muse on
men 'Wasting the earth, each other to destroy'. The spectacle of
solidarity—of unity under a leader—is to be found in hell, and
nowhere on the earth familiar to Milton.

Interlude in Hell

After the dissolution of the Stygian council the heralds proclaim its
outcome and the angels disband to pursue the leisure pastimes of
hell. They are attended by the pathos of false hope and each looks
'where he may likeliest find/Truce to his restless thoughts'. Milton's
sympathies are deeply engaged and the plight of the angels is familiar
to human cultures and to personal consciousness; it is for each an
interlude of waiting, 'till his great chief return'.

The games, tournament battles and violent sports owe much to
Greece and to crusading Europe, but they have their analogues in all
societies. The cruelties are savage and infernal, however, in their
more extravagant manifestations, and for these Milton finds analogues
in myth and not in fact (II, 539–46); but the myths themselves are
oblique expressions of human despair and distress. In this turbulent
world, Milton's own kind 'Retreated in a silent valley' sing of defeat
to take 'with ravishment/The thronging audience'. The poem seems
momentarily to reflect upon itself—'For eloquence the soul, song

charms the sense', finding philosophic discourse 'more sweet' than
the songs of 'hapless fall/By doom of battle'. It is not easy to acqui-
esce, for even here the charm of 'song' (II, 546–55) may be thought
to surpass the charm of 'eloquence' (555–69), especially since Milton
is so dismissive of 'false philosophy' in line 565. But in the fallen
state where hell and earth commingle, Milton witnesses to the ironies
of his position: He admires and emulates the pagan heroic poets who
can have no place in his heaven (for there can be no pathos of defeat);
and he respects and studies the ancient philosophers—particularly
the stoics—whose wisdom he must both assimilate and transcend.
Yet he cannot rest satisfied with them—they are only 'Truce to his
restless thoughts'.

Milton is not, however, solely engaged with the poets and philoso-
phers: he is responsive too to those who set out 'On bold adventure
to discover wide/That dismal world'. The symbolic landscapes of
distress are explored in ways that recall the terrestial explorations of the
Renaissance, searching the world for spiritual and material consola-
tions, 'if any clime perhaps,/Might yield them easier habitation'.
But the angels discover only fresh prospects of suffering. In compari-
son with Virgil (*Aeneid* VI) and Spenser (*Faerie Queene* II, vii, viii)
Milton expresses spiritual states as a progress through a nightmare
landscape, with coexistent abstraction, actuality and fantasy. Thus,
in spiritual terms, the prospects of hate, sorrow and lamentation yield
to oblivion; but the symbolic rivers of Virgil and of Revelation
become immediately present to the listening senses, the landscape
grows more actual, and we discover beyond the 'slow and silent
stream of Lethe' a 'frozen continent' where the ice 'Thaws not, but
gathers heap, and ruin seems/Of ancient pile'. We may interpret this
arctic territory as a state of atrophied feeling that waits for those who
long for oblivion but are denied it (II, 604–14); Milton does not
interpret, however; we know the state by a visionary rendering of a
region of the earth. There is indeed much to remind us that the earth
itself offers these afflictive territories and climates; but the oddly
distancing effect of Milton's language prevents us from a response

appropriate to a lurid geography merely. The devils are made, as it were, to undergo all the ordeals available to man, and man and devil seem to meet in the phantasmagoria of the poem: 'Immovable, infix'd, and frozen round,/Periods of time, thence hurried back to fire'. Is this what Sir Thomas Browne called 'corporal affliction', representing hell to 'grosser apprehensions'; or is it a familiar human condition, an oscillation between paralysis and despair?

Sin and Death

If we look for a way of saying what Satan represents in the poem, Milton often supplies the formulations we need. Thus he 'explores his solitary flight' with 'thoughts inflam'd of highest design' (II, 630). That inflamed high thinking seems to sustain the mercantile enterprises of Ternate and Tidore (where on earth are they? we wonder) and the ships 'stemming nightly toward the pole'. We are reminded of the adventurous aspirations of Renaissance voyagers, and of Marlowe's Faustus 'searching all corners of the new-found world'. But the effect of the metaphor is here to compel us to feel more intensely the constriction of hell's 'horrid roof' and ninefold gates, and the horror of the 'formidable shapes, that keep watch on either side. Milton recalls us to the legend of Scylla in Homer and Ovid, one of the twin monsters (the other, of course, Charybdis), that the poets' imaginations had made out of the natural hazards—rocks and whirlpool—of the straits of Messina. There is therefore a distinct allusion to the *Odyssey*, and some continuity between the voyaging in the Spice Islands and Satan's confrontation of the figures at the gates.

The continuity is scarcely resumed, however, until the voyage resumes across the 'dark/Illimitable ocean' in line 892. In the meantime Milton refines and complicates his allegory of Sin and Death. Much is assimilated from Spenser's figure of Error in the *Faerie Queene*:

> And as she lay upon the durtie ground,
> Her huge long taile her den all overspred,
> Yet was in knots and many boughtes upwound,

> Pointed with mortall sting. Of her there bred
> A thousand yong ones, which she dayly fed,
> Sucking upon her poisonous dugs, each one
> Of sundry shapes, yet all ill favored:
> Soon as that uncouth light upon them shone,
> Into her mouth they crept, and suddain all were gone.
>
> (I, i, xv)

Spenser's innocent matter-of-factness conceals a patient concern with his theological theme; Error is heresy, and her breeding here represents the multiplication of heresies from one source; later she will be strangled by Holiness and her vomit will be found full of books and papers. Spenser's leisured, thoughtful embroideries do not stir the blood. Milton's phantoms are designed to shock, for the verse insists on the suffering and violence of unnatural genesis ('Tore through my entrails, that with fear and pain/Distorted'), and the allegory is a cruel parody of the processes of true creation.

If one of Milton's starting-points was the story of Scylla and her hounds (suggested by the yelping of the sea in the straits), the other was a text from the General Epistle of James: 'Then, when lust hath conceived, it bringeth forth sin; and sin, when it is finished, bringeth forth death' (1.15). Thus it happens that Sin springs from Satan's head (like Athena from the head of Zeus) just as he conceives his 'bold conspiracy against heaven's king'. The nauseating procreative couplings that follow (father upon daughter and son upon daughter) begin auspiciously (761–67) if ironically ('Thyself in me thy perfect image viewing'), but end in mutual and general revulsion (e.g. 785–807). Milton creates unions and antipathies from the uglier human experiences of birth, copulation and death (pain, rape, corruption); and like the fantastic births and rebirths, revulsions keep 'bursting forth afresh' until the imagination is satiated. But as in much Baroque art, there is enjoyment in the macabre virtuosity and we may respond accordingly.

Satan's urbanity (815 ff.) is remarkable in the circumstances('Dear

daughter' and 'fair son') and the span of his ambitions can encompass
Sin and Death with tender solicitude (840–4). But the privileges
that Satan offers his family cannot be theirs unless Sin opens the
gates of hell. Sin's case for obeying Satan rather than God (850–70)
seems irresistible (what has she to lose?) but it is without significant
moral or theological content. It is nevertheless just possible to recog-
nise in Sin's domestic and political ambitions (865–70) the beginnings
of an 'infernal Trinity' of Satan, Sin and Death—a parody that is not
fully sustained (cf. note on II, 747 ff.).

The Realm of Chaos

As already observed, the involvement of earth with hell reaches
us as a part of Satan's design (II, 383–5) and as an element in our
experience of the poem. In the last phase of Book II it is accomplished
in the imagined architecture of the cosmos. The gates of hell open
upon the 'hoary deep', a phrase borrowed from a text in Job which
may more comprehensively have haunted Milton's imagination:
'He maketh a path to shine after him; one would think the deep to
be hoary' (41.32).

Satan's track across the void is in part a continuing Odyssey, on
'sail-broad vans' in 'audacious' flight, like Jason's *Argo* through the
Bosphorus and like Ulysses past Charybdis (1017–20), until with
'shrouds and tackle torn' he comes in sight of the 'empyreal heav'n'
and its 'pendent world'. But heroic voyaging is not the only kind
of movement. There is the 'gryphon through the wilderness' (943),
the lonely figure struggling with imperfect dignity but desperate
eagerness 'o'er bog or steep, through straight, rough, dense, or rare'
(949), and there is the 'pyramid of fire' in the wild expanse of fighting
elements (1013–15). The differing energies of movement are drama-
tised versions of those that sustain 'specious deeds on earth, which
glory excites' (II, 484), and they invite qualified admiration.

Paradise Lost, like the Book of Genesis, is much concerned with
the generation of life out of fragmentary, chaotic elements. It is

therefore appropriate that the allegory of Sin and Death, with its tormented breeding, should be followed by the searching of the 'wild abyss,/The womb of nature and perhaps her grave' (910–11). Milton takes over from Hesiod the myth of 'eldest Night and Chaos' and assimilates it into his version of the Hebraic story. Perpetual conflict in a void is made to appear a cosmic principle and a psychological: the contending elements 'hot, cold, moist and dry' strive for mastery both in the abyss and in the human consciousness, but Milton makes the point wryly with glimpses of earthly 'flags', 'faction' and 'clans' (901); and he takes other opportunities to relate the mess of the 'wasteful deep' to the messes of the human world (965–67). There remains, nevertheless, a powerful conviction that the dark materials of the abyss can be ordained for fresh creation (913–14). The creative energies of both Milton and Satan are engaged in finding heroic words, conviction, emotion and movement in a state of 'tumult and confusion all embroil'd'. The chaos which waits for the ordinance of God, however, an exhausting formless discord adjoining a 'vast vacuity' (932), remains as an image of unheroic evil. The Manichean potential of the poem, therefore, which allows stature to the Prince of Darkness—courtly and invincible in his own terrain—is contrained by the self-negating miseries of the realm he seeks to extend. The poem is ultimately consistent with that Christian view of evil which sees it as a complex of absences—of form, order, light, significance and love. But that 'ultimate' is remote and mysterious. The ancient disintegrating figure of Anarch ('With falt'ring speech and visage incompos'd') is Satan's guide merely, not his master. The metaphoric prospect of a 'banner'd host/Under spread ensigns' passing through the gates of hell (885–6) relates to the 'broad and beaten way' and 'bridge of wondrous length' that Sin and Death carry to 'th' utmost orb of this frail world'. The way that was arduously opened is amply and easily maintained. 'Such was the will of heav'n' says Milton (1025), reminding us that Satan's energies and enterprise have divine consent and are consummated within God's design. For an understanding of that design a full experience

of Books I and II is essential—the descending and reascending of which
Milton speaks in retrospect at the start of Book III:

> Thee I revisit now with bolder wing,
> Escap'd the Stygian pool, though long detain'd
> In that obscure sojourn, while in my flight
> Through utter and through middle darkness borne
> With other notes than to th' Orphean lyre
> I sung of Chaos and eternal Night,
> Taught by the heav'nly Muse to venture down
> The dark descent, and up to reascend,
> Though hard and rare.
>
> (III, 13–21)

Milton's character, conviction and spacious imagination are tem-
pered by 'dark descent' and, in the further reaches of the poem,
will find new ways of ascending.

Paradise Lost

🙝🙝🙝🙝🙝🙝🙝🙝🙝🙝🙝🙝🙝🙝🙝🙝🙝🙝🙝🙝🙝🙝🙝🙝🙝🙝🙝🙝🙝🙝🙝🙝🙝🙝🙝🙝🙝🙝

The Verse[1]

The measure is English heroic verse without rhyme, as that of Homer in Greek, and of Virgil in Latin; rhyme being no necessary adjunct or true ornament of poem or good verse, in longer works especially, but the invention of a barbarous age, to set off wretched matter and lame metre; graced indeed since by the use of some famous modern poets, carried away by custom, but much to their own vexation, hindrance, and constraint to express many things otherwise, and for the most part worse than else they would have expressed them. Not without cause therefore some both Italian and Spanish poets of prime note have rejected rhyme both in longer and shorter works, as have also long since our best English tragedies, as a thing of itself, to all judicious ears, trivial and of no true musical delight; which consists only in apt numbers, fit quantity of syllables, and the sense variously drawn out from one verse into another, not in the jingling sound of like endings, a fault avoided by the learned ancients both in poetry and all good oratory. This neglect then of rhyme so little is to be taken for a defect, though it may seem so perhaps to vulgar readers, that it rather is to be esteemed an example set, the first in English, of ancient liberty recovered to heroic poem from the troublesome and modern bondage of rhyming.

[1] Added by Milton in 1668, within a year of the poem's first appearance. The explanation 'why the poem rhymes not' was written, we are told by his publisher, 'For the satisfaction of many that have desired it'. The 'Arguments' or prose summaries are also Milton's; initially grouped together, they were later (1674) apportioned to the twelve books.

The Arguments of Books I—XII

I—II

(See below, pp. 85 and 139)

III

God sitting on his throne sees Satan flying towards this world, then
newly created; shows him to the Son who sat at his right hand;
foretells the success of Satan in perverting mankind; clears his own
justice and wisdom from all imputation, having created man free
and able enough to have withstood his tempter; yet declares his
purpose of grace towards him, in regard he fell not of his own malice,
as did Satan, but by him seduced. The Son of God renders praise
to his Father for the manifestation of his gracious purpose towards
man; but God again declares, that grace cannot be extended toward
man without the satisfaction of divine justice; man hath offended
the majesty of God by aspiring to Godhead, and therefore with all
his progeny devoted to death must die, unless some one can be found
sufficient to answer for his offence, and undergo his punishment.
The Son of God freely offers himself a ransom for man: the Father
accepts him, ordains his incarnation, pronounces his exaltation above
all names in heaven and earth; commands all the angels to adore
him; they obey, and hymning to their harps in full choir, celebrate
the Father and the Son. Meanwhile Satan alights upon the bare
convex of this world's outermost orb; where wandering he first
finds a place since called the Limbo of Vanity; what persons and
things fly up thither; thence comes to the gate of heaven, described
ascending by stairs, and the waters above the firmament that flow
about it: his passage thence to the orb of the sun; he finds there
Uriel the regent of that orb, but first changes himself into the shape

of a meaner angel; and pretending a zealous desire to behold the new creation and man whom God had placed here, inquires of him the place of his habitation, and is directed; alights first on Mount Niphates.

IV

Satan now in prospect of Eden, and nigh the place where he must now attempt the bold enterprise which he undertook alone against God and man, falls into many doubts with himself, and many passions, fear, envy, and despair; but at length confirms himself in evil, journeys on to Paradise, whose outward prospect and situation is described, overleaps the bounds, sits in the shape of a cormorant on the tree of life, as the highest in the garden to look about him. The garden described; Satan's first sight of Adam and Eve, his wonder at their excellent form and happy state, but with resolution to work their fall; overhears their discourse, thence gathers that the tree of knowledge was forbidden them to eat of, under penalty of death; and thereon intends to found his temptation, by seducing them to transgress: then leaves them a while to know farther of their state by some other means. Meanwhile, Uriel descending on a sunbeam warns Gabriel, who had in charge the gate of Paradise, that some evil spirit had escaped the deep, and passed at noon by his sphere in the shape of a good angel down to Paradise, discovered after by his furious gestures in the mount. Gabriel promises to find him ere morning. Night coming on, Adam and Eve discourse of going to their rest: their bower described; their evening worship. Gabriel drawing forth his bands of night-watch to walk the round of Paradise, appoints two strong angels to Adam's bower, lest the evil spirit should be there doing some harm to Adam or Eve sleeping; there they find him at the ear of Eve, tempting her in a dream, and bring him, though unwilling, to Gabriel; by whom questioned, he scornfully answers, prepares resistance, but hindered by a sign from heaven, flies out of Paradise.

V

Morning approached, Eve relates to Adam her troublesome dream:
he likes it not, yet comforts her: they come forth to their day
labours: their morning hymn at the door of their bower. God to ren-
der man inexcusable sends Raphael to admonish him of his obedience,
of his free estate, of his enemy near at hand; who he is, and why his
enemy, and whatever else may avail Adam to know. Raphael comes
down to Paradise, his appearance described, his coming discerned
by Adam afar off sitting at the door of his bower; he goes out to
meet him, brings him to his lodge, entertains him with the choicest
fruits of Paradise got together by Eve; their discourse at table:
Raphael performs his message, minds Adams of his state and of his
enemy: relates at Adam's request who that enemy is, and how he
came to be so, beginning from his first revolt in heaven, and the
occasion thereof; how he drew his legions after him to the parts of
the north, and there incited them to rebel with him, persuading all
but only Abdiel, a seraph, who in argument dissuades and opposes
him, then forsakes him.

VI

Raphael continues to relate how Michael and Gabriel were sent forth
to battle against Satan and his angels. The first fight described;
Satan and his powers retire under night: he calls a council, invents
devilish engines, which in the second day's fight put Michael and
his angels to some disorder; but they at length pulling up mountains
overwhelm both the force and machines of Satan: yet the tumult
not so ending, God on the third day sends Messiah his Son, for whom
he had reserved the glory of that victory: he in the power of his
Father coming to the place, and causing all his legions to stand still
on either side, with his chariot and thunder driving into the midst
of his enemies, pursues them unable to resist towards the wall of

heaven; which opening, they leap down with horror and confusion
into the place of punishment prepared for them in the deep: Messiah
returns with triumph to his Father.

VII

Raphael at the request of Adam relates how and wherefore this world
was first created; that God, after the expelling of Satan and his angels
out of heaven, declared his pleasure to create another world and
other creatures to dwell therein; sends his Son with glory and atten-
dance of angels to perform the work of creation in six days: the
angels celebrate with hymns the performance thereof, and his re-
ascension into heaven.

VIII

Adam inquires concerning celestial motions, is doubtfully answered,
and exhorted to search rather things more worthy of knowledge.
Adam assents, and still desirous to detain Raphael, relates to him what
he remembered since his own creation, his placing in Paradise, his
talk with God concerning solitude and fit society, his first meeting
and nuptials with Eve, his discourse with the angel thereupon; who
after admonitions repeated departs.

IX

Satan having compassed the earth, with meditated guile returns as a
mist by night into Paradise, enters into the serpent sleeping. Adam
and Eve in the morning go forth to their labours, which Eve pro-
poses to divide in several places, each labouring apart: Adam consents
not, alleging the danger, lest that enemy, of whom they were fore-

warned, should attempt her found alone: Eve loth to be thought not circumspect or firm enough, urges her going apart, the rather desirous to make trial of her strength; Adam at last yields: the serpent finds her alone; his subtle approach, first gazing, then speaking, with much flattery extolling Eve above all other creatures. Eve wondering to hear the serpent speak, asks how he attained to human speech and such understanding not till now; the serpent answers, that by tasting of a certain tree in the garden he attained both to speech and reason, till then void of both: Eve requires him to bring her to that tree, and finds it to be the tree of knowledge forbidden: the serpent now grown bolder, with many wiles and arguments induces her at length to eat; she pleased with the taste deliberates a while whether to impart thereof to Adam or not, at last brings him of the fruit, relates what persuaded her to eat thereof: Adam at first amazed, but perceiving her lost, resolves through vehemence of love to perish with her; and extenuating the trespass eats also of the fruit: the effects thereof in them both; they seek to cover their nakedness; then fall to variance and accusation of one another.

X

Man's transgression known, the guardian angels forsake Paradise, and return up to heaven to approve their vigilance, and are approved, God declaring that the entrance of Satan could not be by them prevented. He sends his Son to judge the transgressors, who descends and gives sentence accordingly; then in pity clothes them both, and re-ascends. Sin and Death sitting till then at the gates of hell, by wondrous sympathy feeling the success of Satan in this new world, and the sin by man there committed, resolve to sit no longer confined in hell, but to follow Satan their sire up to the place of man: to make the way easier from hell to this world to and fro, they pave a broad highway or bridge over Chaos, according to the track that Satan first made; then preparing for earth, they meet him proud of his success returning to hell; their mutual gratulation. Satan arrives at Pandemonium, in full assembly relates with boasting his success against man; instead of applause is entertained with a general hiss by all his audience, transformed with himself also suddenly into serpents, according to his doom given in Paradise; then deluded with a show of the forbidden tree springing up before them, they greedily reaching to take of the fruit, chew dust and bitter ashes. The proceedings of Sin and Death; God foretells the final victory of his Son over them, and the renewing of all things; but for the present commands his angels to make several alterations in the heavens and elements. Adam more and more perceiving his fallen condition heavily bewails, rejects the condolement of Eve; she persists and at length appeases him: then to evade the curse likely to fall on their offspring, proposes to Adam violent ways which he approves not, but conceiving better hope, puts her in mind of the late promise made them, that her seed should be revenged on the serpent, and exhorts her with him to seek peace of the offended Deity, by repentance and supplication.

XI

The Son of God presents to his Father the prayers of our first parents now repenting, and intercedes for them: God accepts them, but declares that they must no longer abide in Paradise; sends Michael with a band of cherubim to dispossess them; but first to reveal to Adam future things: Michael's coming down. Adam shows to Eve certain ominous signs: he discerns Michael's approach, goes out to meet him: the angel denounces their departure. Eve's lamentation. Adam pleads, but submits; the angel leads him up to a high hill, sets before him in vision what shall happen till the Flood.

XII

The angel Michael continues from the Flood to relate what shall succeed; then, in the mention of Abraham, comes by degrees to explain, who that seed of the woman shall be, which was promised Adam and Eve in the Fall; his incarnation, death, resurrection, and ascension; the state of the Church till his second coming. Adam greatly satisfied and recomforted by these relations and promises descends the hill with Michael; wakens Eve, who all this while had slept, but with gentle dreams composed to quietness of mind and submission. Michael in either hand leads them out of Paradise, the fiery sword waving behind them, and the cherubim taking their stations to guard the place.

The concluding lines:

> In either hand the hast'ning angel caught
> Our ling'ring parents, and to th' eastern gate
> Led them direct, and down the cliff as fast
> To the subjected plain; then disappear'd.
> They looking back, all th' eastern side beheld
> Of Paradise, so late their happy seat,
> Wav'd over by that flaming brand, the gate
> With dreadful faces throng'd and fiery arms:
> Some natural tears they dropp'd, but wip'd them soon;
> The world was all before them, where to choose
> Their place of rest, and providence their guide:
> They hand in hand with wand'ring steps and slow,
> Through Eden took their solitary way.

Paradise Lost
Books I—II

NOTES

the poem hastes into the midst of things The action of *Paradise Lost*, like that of *The Iliad* or *The Aeneid*, begins according to established custom *in medias res*. Milton will initially outline what preceded the opening scene of 'Satan with his angels now fallen into hell' (see below, 36–53), reserving for Books V–VI a fuller account of Satan's rebellion and fall from heaven.

hell, describ'd here, not in the centre i.e., not at the centre of the universe, much less of the earth. See 'The Universe of *Paradise Lost*' below, pp. 213 ff.

heaven and earth may be suppos'd as yet not made The universe was created, after the fall of Satan, from a pre-existent chaos (fully described later, in II, 890–916). 'Heaven' here means the skies, not the abode of God (= empyrean).

a new world and new kind of creature to be created, according to an ancient prophesy or report Cf. the rumour ('fame') mentioned in I, 650–4, and repeated in II, 345 ff.

The Argument of Book I

This first book proposes, first in brief, the whole subject, man's disobedience, and the loss thereupon of Paradise wherein he was placed: then touches the prime cause of his fall, the serpent, or rather Satan in the serpent; who revolting from God, and drawing to his side many legions of angels, was by the command of God driven out of heaven with all his crew into the great deep. Which action passed over, the poem hastes into the midst of things, presenting Satan with his angels now fallen into hell, described here, not in the centre (for heaven and earth may be supposed as yet not made, certainly not yet accursed) but in a place of utter darkness, fitliest called Chaos: here Satan with his angels lying on the burning lake, thunderstruck and astonished, after a certain space recovers, as from confusion, calls up him who next in order and dignity lay by him; they confer of their miserable fall. Satan awakens all his legions, who lay till then in the same manner confounded; they rise, their numbers, array of battle, their chief leaders named, according to the idols known afterwards in Canaan and the countries adjoining. To these Satan directs his speech, comforts them with hope yet of regaining heaven, but tells them lastly of a new world and new kind of creature to be created, according to an ancient prophecy or report in heaven; for that angels were long before this visible creation, was the opinion of many ancient Fathers. To find out the truth of this prophecy, and what to determine thereon, he refers to a full council. What his associates thence attempt. Pandemonium the palace of Satan rises, suddenly built out of the deep: the infernal peers there sit in council.

1 ff. Milton's conscious imitation of classical precedents is made explicit in the first instance through the use of epic 'conventions'. The *principium* (1–26) outlines the poem's action in imitation of Homer's *Iliad* (1–7) and Virgil's *Aeneid* (1–7). The *invocatio* (1–49) is an address to the Muse similar to Homer's (8–16) and Virgil's (8–33).

1–5 Milton's emphasis on 'man' is similar to Homer's as well as Virgil's, yet different in that he posits 'one greater man'—Christ. Cf. Romans 5.19. A poem in the classical tradition, therefore, is swiftly placed within a Christian context.

6 ff. heav'nly Muse Milton again follows Homer and Virgil in addressing the Muse, yet again differs from them by invoking not a muse from the pagan pantheon but a power which is expressly identified with the inspirer of Moses. This power is later named Urania, 'the heavenly one' (VII, 1–12).

6   secret possibly from the Latin *secretus*, solitary, apart

7   Oreb (Horeb) and **Sinai** Moses saw the vision of the burning bush in the first, and received the Law atop the second.

8   That shepherd Moses **the chosen seed** the Israelites. The momentous events outlined here and more fully set forth later, are repeatedly stressed at the outset through the reiterated word *first*.

9   In the beginning etc. Moses was believed to have been the author of the account of creation in Genesis whose opening phrase is quoted here.

10   Sion the sacred hill of the Jews, analogous to Mount Helicon (see 14–15).

11   Siloa's brook the pool at the foot of Mount Sion, analogous to Aganippes the holy spring of the Greek Muses

12   the oracle of God see the Introduction, above, p. 32.

14–15   intends to soar etc. the metaphor—a favourite of Milton's—is not mere bravado. The flight above **th' Aonian mount** (Helicon, the sacred hill of the Greek Muses) not only affirms the 'high' style of *Paradise Lost*; it also insists on the moral superiority of Milton's subject.

15   pursues treats of (cf. the Latin *sequor*)

17–23 The prayer to the Holy Spirit for guidance asserts also the divine ability to create—and so to invert, in due course, the 'mortal taste' of the forbidden fruit (1–2). The metaphoric significance of **pregnant** (22) becomes apparent when contrasted to the sterility of hell and its inhabitants.

21   Dove-like etc. the Holy Spirit is often represented as a dove, on the basis of His appearance at the baptism of Christ (Luke 3.22). **abyss** chaos

24   argument subject (the Latin *argumentum*)

26   justify the ways of God to men demonstrate the justice of God's ways, not so much logically as spiritually

27–49 Another epic 'convention' used by Milton is the *initium* which states the cause of the poem's action. Cf. *The Iliad* 1–7, and *The Aeneid* 8–11.

Book I

🙚🙚🙚🙚🙚🙚🙚🙚🙚🙚🙚🙚🙚🙚🙚🙚🙚🙚🙚🙚🙚🙚🙚🙚🙚🙚🙚🙚🙚🙚🙚🙚🙚🙚🙚🙚

Of man's first disobedience, and the fruit ~ *begins poem ½ way.*
Of that forbidden tree, whose mortal taste
Brought death into the world, and all our woe,
With loss of Eden, till one greater man
Restore us, and regain the blissful seat,   5
Sing heav'nly Muse, that on the secret top   *heart nor church = seat of interpretation.*
Of Oreb, or of Sinai, didst inspire
That shepherd, who first taught the chosen seed,
In the beginning how the heav'ns and earth
Rose out of chaos: Or if Sion hill   10
Delight thee more, and Siloa's brook that flow'd
Fast by the oracle of God; I thence   *fusion of relig*
Invoke thy aid to my advent'rous song,   *purpose &*
That with no middle flight intends to soar   *poetic inspiration*   *of style or subject*
Above th' Aonian mount, while it pursues   15
Things unattempted yet in prose or rhyme.   *moral superiority*
And chiefly thou O Spirit, that dost prefer
Before all temples th' upright heart and pure,   *syntax*
Instruct me, for thou know'st; thou from the first
Wast present, and with mighty wings outspread *eagle + dove - great but gentle.*   20
Dove-like sat'st brooding on the vast abyss
And mad'st it pregnant: What in me is dark ~ *was bird - female - vision produced?*
Illumine, what is low raise and support;
That to the highth of this great argument
I may assert eternal providence,   25
And justify the ways of God to men.

Say first, for heav'n hides nothing from thy view
Show men the drama from which he must choose.

28 the deep tract of hell See the Introduction, above, p. 50 ff.
29 grand original; also general or all-inclusive

33–4 For a similar question and answer, see *The Iliad* I, 8.
34 Cf. Revelation 20.2: 'that old serpent, which is the Devil, and Satan'

36 what time at which time (the Latin *quo tempore*)

39 peers equals (the Latin *pares*)
40 ff. Among the numerous Biblical allusions compressed here are Isaiah
14.9–17 (quoted above, pp. 47–8, Jude, 6, Revelation 20.1–2, etc.

44 With vain attempt See below, II, 9.
45 flaming Cf. Luke 10.18: 'I beheld Satan as lightning fall from heaven.'
46 combustion continues the metaphor of the previous line but expressly
suggests 'confusion'

48 adamantine chains made of 'adamant', by Milton's time understood
in the sense of 'as hard as diamond'. The chains are not to be taken literally;
as is common with Milton, physical objects all too often intimate spiritual
states of mind (cf. the Introduction, above, pp. 69–70). Satan like all his
disciples is left 'at large to his own dark designs' (213), confined not so much
by any actual chains as by his own passions.
50–83 The epic 'convention' of the *exordium* introduces us to the poem's
action. Cf. *Iliad*, 8 ff., and *Aeneid*, 12 ff.
50 Nine days also lasted the fall of the Titans (Hesiod, *Theogony*, 722). The
allusion prepares us among other things for Milton's equation of the fallen
angels with the idols and deities of the pre-Christian era (364–75). It also
anticipates the first epic simile (197 ff.).
56 baleful full of woe but also of evil
57 witness'd bore witness to
58 obdurate scanned 'obdúrate'

Nor the deep tract of hell, say first what cause
Mov'd our grand parents in that happy state,
Favour'd of heav'n so highly, to fall off   30
From their creator, and transgress his will
For one restraint, lords of the world besides?
Who first seduc'd them to that foul revolt?
Th' infernal serpent; he it was, whose guile
Stirr'd up with envy and revenge, deceiv'd   35
The mother of mankind, what time his pride
Had cast him out from heav'n, with all his host
Of rebel angels, by whose aid aspiring
To set himself in glory above his peers,
He trusted to have equall'd the most high,   40
If he oppos'd; and with ambitious aim
Against the throne and monarchy of God
Rais'd impious war in heav'n and battle proud
With vain attempt. Him the almighty power
Hurl'd headlong flaming from th' ethereal sky   45
With hideous ruin and combustion down
To bottomless perdition, there to dwell
In adamantine chains and penal fire,
Who durst defy th' omnipotent to arms.
Nine times the space that measures day and night   50
To mortal men, he with his horrid crew
Lay vanquish'd, rolling in the fiery gulf
Confounded though immortal: but his doom
Reserv'd him to more wrath; for now the thought
Both of lost happiness and lasting pain   55
Torments him; round he throws his baleful eyes
That witness'd huge affliction and dismay
Mix'd with obdurate pride and steadfast hate:

59 ken (a verb, not a noun) can see. Cf. 2 *Henry VI* III, ii, 101: 'As far as I could ken thy chalky cliffs'.

63 darkness visible the oxymoron attempts to affirm the tradition of hell's flames in a realm said to be 'a land of darkness, as darkness itself . . ., and where the light is as darkness' (Job 10.22). Cf. 181–3. As always, however, Milton is also venturing a moral judgement by emphasising the incongruous, unnatural and perverse nature of hell.

66 hope never comes Cf. the inscription over the gate of hell in Dante's *Inferno*, III, 9: 'Abandon hope all you who enter here.'

68 urges afflicts (the Latin *urgere*)

72 utter utter (in the sense of 'complete') but also 'outer'

74 The distance between hell and heaven is thrice the distance between the earth (**the centre**) and the outermost shell or sphere of the universe. The calculation is of course important symbolically.

78 welt'ring rolling on the lake's surface

81 Beëlzebub literally 'Lord of the Flies', a sun-god of the Philistines, is assigned by Milton to a position of authority second only to that of Satan. Cf. II, 299.

82 Satan literally 'adversary', who after his fall from heaven was no longer de.ignated by his former name Lucifer. Cf. 361–3.

84 beest another form of 'art' **O how fall'n! how chang'd** the allusion is to Isaiah 14.12 ('How art thou fallen from heaven, O Lucifer, son of the morning!') and to *The Aeneid* II, 275–6 ('Hei mihi qualis erat! quantum mutatus ab illo/Hectore qui redit')

85 the happy realms of light the most grievous loss experienced by the fallen angels is their sense of deprivation of heaven's light. Physical pain is by no means absent (cf. II, 599) but is certainly of secondary importance. Cf. Mephistophiles in Marlowe's *Doctor Faustus* 312–16:

> Why, this is hell, nor am I out of it:
> Think'st thou that I who saw the face of God,
> And tasted the eternal joys of Heaven,
> Am not tormented with ten thousand hells,
> In being deprived of everlasting bliss?

87 if he if thou beest he (as in 84)

At once as far as angels ken he views
The dismal situation waste and wild,   60
A dungeon horrible, on all sides round
As one great furnace flam'd, yet from those flames
No light, but rather darkness visible
Serv'd only to discover sights of woe,
Regions of sorrow, doleful shades, where peace   65
And rest can never dwell, hope never comes
That comes to all; but torture without end
Still urges, and a fiery deluge, fed
With ever-burning sulphur unconsum'd:
Such place eternal justice had prepar'd   70
For those rebellious, here their prison ordain'd
In utter darkness, and their portion set
As far remov'd from God and light of heav'n
As from the centre thrice to th' utmost pole.
O how unlike the place from whence they fell!   75
There the companions of his fall, o'erwhelm'd
With floods and whirlwinds of tempestuous fire,
He soon discerns, and welt'ring by his side
One next himself in power, and next in crime,
Long after known in Palestine, and nam'd   80
Beëlzebub. To whom th' arch-enemy,
And thence in heav'n call'd Satan, with bold words
Breaking the horrid silence thus began.
  If thou beest he; but O how fall'n! how chang'd
From him, who in the happy realms of light   85
Cloth'd with transcendent brightness didst outshine
Myriads though bright: if he whom mutual league,
United thoughts and counsels, equal hope
And hazard in the glorious enterprise,

90 Join'd The subjects of this verb are 'league', 'thoughts and counsels', 'hope' and 'hazard'.

93 his thunder Details of the war in heaven occur throughout Books I and II, well in advance of Milton's full account in Book VI. Here Satan and his disciples present their own interpretation of the war, inevitably much distorted. It will be noted that nearly all avoid naming God directly.

94–7 Equally defiant statements are made by the hero of Aeschylus in *Prometheus Bound* 987–96, and by Capaneus in Dante's *Inferno* XIV, 52–91.

96 else in addition

98 sense of injur'd merit the nominal cause of Satan's rebellion in heaven is later said to have been his violent disapproval of the elevation of the Son of God over himself (V, 772 ff.). Satan's notion of 'merit' is sharply contrasted to that of the Son who is 'By merit more than birthright Son of God' (III, 309), and 'by right of merit reigns' (VI, 43).

104 dubious because the war in heaven appeared to have been in doubt for three days. The point of view is strictly Satan's own.

105 shook his throne A false boast, as Milton later makes clear (VI, 833–4).

107 study of pursuit of (the Latin *studium*, exertion, endeavour)

114 Doubted (feared for) **his empire** another deliberate falsehood

115 ignominy possibly pronounced 'ignomy'

116 by fate Here and elsewhere Satan insists on positing a higher power than God. Significantly, Moloch and Belial do not share this point of view (II, 92 ff., 142 ff.), and Satan's premise is denied altogether in God's subsequent words, 'What I will is fate' (VII, 173).

117 empyreal literally 'made of fire'. Satan's claim that the 'fiery' element of their substance is imperishable fails to convince his disciples (cf. II, 99, 146–54).

120 successful hope hope of success

Join'd with me once, now misery hath join'd   90
In equal ruin: into what pit thou seest
From what highth fall'n, so much the stronger prov'd
He with his thunder: and till then who knew
The force of those dire arms? yet not for those,
Nor what the potent victor in his rage   95
Can else inflict, do I repent or change,
Though chang'd in outward lustre; that fix'd mind
And high disdain, from sense of injur'd merit,
That with the mightiest rais'd me to contend,
And to the fierce contention brought along   100
Innumerable force to spirits arm'd
That durst dislike his reign, and me preferring,
His utmost power with adverse power oppos'd
In dubious battle on the plains of heav'n,
And shook his throne. What though the field be lost? 105
All is not lost; th' unconquerable will,
And study of revenge, immortal hate,
And courage never to submit or yield:
And what is else not to be overcome?
That glory never shall his wrath or might   110
Extort from me. To bow and sue for grace
With suppliant knee, and deify his power,
Who from the terror of this arm so late
Doubted his empire, that were low indeed,
That were an ignominy and shame beneath   115
This downfall; since by fate the strength of gods
And this empyreal substance cannot fail,
Since through experience of this great event
In arms not worse, in foresight much advanc'd,
We may with more successful hope resolve   120

121 by force or guile Satan already limits the nature of the forthcoming debate in Book II.

124 tyranny Satan's point of view will again be corrected later through an emphasis on his free will which is acknowledged even by himself (IV, 71–2).

128 ff. The aroused Beëlzebub begins confidently enough, and willingly permits himself the illusion that the war in heaven had 'endanger'd' its 'perpetual' (but not 'eternal') King. Observe, however, how swiftly he sinks into despair, which prompts Satan's 'speedy words' (156).

129 seraphim The plural of 'seraph', one of the orders of angels. Cf. 'cherub' (157), whence 'cherubim'.

144 Of force of necessity, perforce

149–52 Ironically, Beëlzebub anticipates the role hereafter assigned to the fallen angels by God. As Milton wrote in his theological treatise *De Doctrina Christiana*: 'They are sometimes permitted to wander throughout the whole earth, the air, and heaven itself, to execute the judgements of God.'

To wage by force or guile eternal war
Irreconcileable, to our grand foe,
Who now triumphs, and in th' excess of joy
Sole reigning holds the tyranny of heav'n.
    So spake th' apostate angel, though in pain,   125
Vaunting aloud, but rack'd with deep despair:
And him thus answer'd soon his bold compeer.
    O prince, O chief of many throned powers,
That led th' embattl'd seraphim to war
Under thy conduct, and in dreadful deeds   130
Fearless, endanger'd heav'n's perpetual king;
And put to proof his high supremacy,
Whether upheld by strength, or chance, or fate,
Too well I see and rue the dire event,
That with sad overthrow and foul defeat   135
Hath lost us heav'n, and all this mighty host
In horrible destruction laid thus low,
As far as gods and heav'nly essences
Can perish: for the mind and spirit remains
Invincible, and vigour soon returns,   140
Though all our glory extinct, and happy state
Here swallow'd up in endless misery.
But what if he our conqueror (whom I now
Of force believe almighty, since no less
Than such could have o'erpow'r'd such force as ours),   145
Have left us this our spirit and strength entire
Strongly to suffer and support our pains,
That we may so suffice his vengeful ire,
Or do him mightier service as his thralls
By right of war, whate'er his business be   150
Here in the heart of hell to work in fire,

152   gloomy deep the realm of Chaos

163   to bring forth good precisely the purpose of God, as demonstrated by Milton in man's creation and, later, in his redemption

167   if I fail not if I am not mistaken

169–71 This detail of the aftermath of the war in heaven is confirmed later (II, 997–8). Significantly, God's 'ministers of vengeance'—i.e. the loyal angels—remained immune from evil even though in hell.

175   red lightning cf. note on II, 174

178   slip let slip

181–3 See above, note on 63.

Or do his errands in the gloomy deep;
What can it then avail though yet we feel
Strength undiminish'd, or eternal being
To undergo eternal punishment?   155
Whereto with speedy words th' arch-fiend repli'd.

  Fall'n cherub, to be weak is miserable
Doing or suffering: but of this be sure,
To do aught good never will be our task,
But ever to do ill our sole delight,   160
As being the contrary to his high will
Whom we resist. If then his providence
Out of our evil seek to bring forth good,
Our labour must be to pervert that end,
And out of good still to find means of evil;   165
Which oft-times may succeed, so as perhaps
Shall grieve him, if I fail not, and disturb
His inmost counsels from their destin'd aim.
But see the angry victor hath recall'd
His ministers of vengeance and pursuit   170
Back to the gates of heav'n: the sulphurous hail
Shot after us in storm, o'erblown hath laid
The fiery surge, that from the precipice
Of heav'n receiv'd us falling, and the thunder,
Wing'd with red lightning and impetuous rage,   175
Perhaps hath spent his shafts, and ceases now
To bellow through the vast and boundless deep.
Let us not slip th' occasion, whether scorn,
Or satiate fury yield it from our foe.
Seest thou yon dreary plain, forlorn and wild,   180
The seat of desolation, void of light,
Save what the glimmering of these livid flames

186 afflicted overthrown, down cast (the Latin *affligere*)

191 resolution from despair See the Introduction, above, p. 54 ff.
193 uplift uplifted
196 rood a unit of land measure
197–208 The first of the great 'epic' similes of *Paradise Lost* is like every other intimately related to the action and to Milton's sustained moral judgements. The Titans and the Giants, however confused their passage through mythology, were rebels against the established gods. The elder Titans, offspring of Ge (Earth: hence 'Earth-born') and Uranus (Heaven), rebelled against their father and enthroned Saturn; but Saturn's son Jupiter (Jove) in turn rose in rebellion against his father and drove the Titans to Hell (Tartarus). The Giants—'Earth-born' like the Titans—were rebels against Jupiter who destroyed them for their ambition; the war involved **Briareos,** a Giant or Titan with a hundred arms, and **Typhon** or Typhoeus, a monster with a hundred serpent-heads (born in a cave in Cilicia of which **ancient Tarsus** was the capital). The series of allusions extends next to the whale-like monster **Leviathan** whose submerged form was said to deceive seamen—precisely as Satan can deceive by a logic which is merely apparent, not real (cf. 'Semblance of worth, not substance', in 529). Milton's warning is enforced by the traditional association of the whale with Satan, and of the leviathan with 'the crooked serpent' (Isaiah 27.1), in turn related by Milton to the serpent-headed Typhon and so to the series of allusions to the rebels against authority. The cumulative insistence on the monstrous perversion of nature carries its own moral judgement, as before (63).
202 ocean Stream a Homeric phrase (ῥόος ὠκεάνοιο)
204 night-founder'd benighted
206 scaly Students of natural history may well protest that whales have no scales; but it could be argued that Milton's unnatural monster combines the whale's size and the crocodile's scales. Significantly, Sin's form ends in 'many a scaly fold' (II, 651).
208 Invests wraps
210 Chain'd etc. See above, note on 48.
212 permission Milton endorses the theory of 'permissive' evil, whereby God allows the wicked to advance to their destruction. The statement is also an answer to the questions raised by Beëlzebub and Satan earlier (143 ff., 157 ff.).

Casts pale and dreadful? Thither let us tend
From off the tossing of these fiery waves,
There rest, if any rest can harbour there,   185
And reassembling our afflicted powers,
Consult how we may henceforth most offend
Our enemy, our own loss how repair,
How overcome this dire calamity,
What reinforcement we may gain from hope,   190
If not what resolution from despair.
  Thus Satan talking to his nearest mate
With head uplift above the wave, and eyes
That sparkling blaz'd, his other parts besides
Prone on the flood, extended long and large   195
Lay floating many a rood, in bulk as huge
As whom the fables name of monstrous size,
Titanian, or Earth-born, that warr'd on Jove,
Briareos or Typhon, whom the den
By ancient Tarsus held, or that sea-beast   200
Leviathan, which God of all his works
Created hugest that swim th' ocean stream:
Him haply slumb'ring on the Norway foam
The pilot of some small night-founder'd skiff,
Deeming some island, oft, as sea-men tell,   205
With fixed anchor in his scaly rind
Moors by his side under the lea, while night
Invests the sea, and wished morn delays:
So stretch'd out huge in length the arch-fiend lay
Chain'd on the burning lake, nor ever thence   210
Had ris'n or heav'd his head, but that the will
And high permission of all-ruling heav'n
Left him at large to his own dark designs,

226 incumbent pressing with his weight

230–7 The terrain is like the floor (**singed bottom**) of a volcano as seen after an eruption. Milton accepts the theory that a volcanic eruption is caused by an earthquake, itself the result of compressed underground winds bursting forth.

232 Pelorus Cape Faro, a promontory near Aetna

235 Sublim'd with mineral fury changed by the intense volcanic heat. Milton as always looks beyond the phenomenon he describes to its moral dimension; the operative word here is, of course, **fury**.

236 involv'd wrapped in (the Latin *involvere*)

239 Stygian infernal. Cf. Styx (literally 'Hate'), the river of Hades (see note on II, 575–81).

240–1 The viewpoint is entirely the devils' own; Milton himself set the record straight in 212 ff.

242 clime region

244 change accept in exchange

sadian

nor a fair fight
sat^n doesn't have a chance

That with reiterated crimes he might
Heap on himself damnation while he sought   215
Evil to others, and enrag'd might see
How all his malice serv'd but to bring forth   PLANNED.
Infinite goodness, grace and mercy shown
On man by him seduc'd, but on himself
Treble confusion, wrath and vengeance pour'd.   220
Forthwith upright he rears from off the pool
His mighty stature; on each hand the flames
Driv'n backward slope their pointing spires, and roll'd
In billows, leave i' th' midst a horrid vale.
Then with expanded wings he steers his flight   225
Aloft, incumbent on the dusky air
That felt unusual weight, till on dry land
He lights, if it were land that ever burn'd
With solid, as the lake with liquid fire;
And such appear'd in hue, as when the force   230
Of subterranean wind transports a hill   *volcano.*
Torn from Pelorus, or the shatter'd side
Of thund'ring Aetna, whose combustible
And fuell'd entrails thence conceiving fire,
Sublim'd with mineral fury, aid the winds,   235
And leave a singed bottom all involv'd
With stench and smoke: such resting found the sole
Of unblest feet. Him followed his next mate,
Both glorying to have scap'd the Stygian flood
As gods, and by their own recover'd strength,   240
Not by the sufferance of supernal power.
  Is this the region, this the soil, the clime,
Said then the lost archangel, this the seat   *Satan*
That we must change for heav'n, this mournful gloom

246 sov'reign Milton's regular spelling is 'sovran'.

248 'Whom force has made supreme but who according to reason is equal'

254-5 As Milton later makes clear, Satan fails to realise this ambition; for
when alone he exclaims:

> Me miserable! which way shall I fly
> Infinite wrath, and infinite despair?
> Which way I fly is hell; myself am hell;
> And in the lowest deep a lower deep
> Still threat'ning to devour me opens wide,
> To which the hell I suffer seems a heav'n.

(IV, 73–8)

257 all but less than nearly equal to. The phrase combines 'only less than'
and 'all but equal to'.

59–60 An example of Satan's conscious irony, to be distinguished from the
irony directed at him (cf. II, 5–9).

66 astonish'd stupefied **oblivious pool** cf. the 'forgetful lake' of II, 74.

For that celestial light? Be it so, since he   245
Who now is sov'reign can dispose and bid
What shall be right: furthest from him is best
Whom reason hath equal'd, force hath made supreme
Above his equals. Farewell happy fields
Where joy for ever dwells: hail horrors, hail   250
Infernal world, and thou profoundest hell
Receive thy new possessor: one who brings
A mind not to be chang'd by place or time.
The mind is its own place, and in itself
Can make a heav'n of hell, a hell of heav'n.   255
What matter where, if I be still the same,
And what I should be, all but less than he
Whom thunder hath made greater? Here at least
We shall be free; th' almighty hath not built
Here for his envy, will not drive us hence: 260
Here we may reign secure, and in my choice
To reign is worth ambition though in hell:
Better to reign in hell, than serve in heav'n.
But wherefore let we then our faithful friends,
Th' associates and copartners of our loss   265
Lie thus astonish'd on th' oblivious pool,
And call them not to share with us their part
In this unhappy mansion, or once more
With rallied arms to try what may be yet
Regain'd in heav'n, or what more lost in hell?   270
   So Satan spake, and him Beëlzebub
Thus answer'd. Leader of those armies bright,
Which but th' omnipotent none could have foil'd,
If once they hear that voice, their liveliest pledge
Of hope in fears and dangers, heard so oft   275

276   edge front line (the Latin *acies*)

282   pernicious destructive (the Latin *perniciosus*)

284-95 Another sustained epic simile, based on several antecedents—for instance the comparison of Achilles' shield to the moon in *The Iliad* XIX, 373, and of the club of Polyphemus to a mast in *The Odyssey* IX, 322. But Satan's shield—tempered in celestial fire (285)—is not merely compared to the moon as seen through Galileo's telescope at **Fesole** near Florence, in the valley of the Arno (**Valdarno**); much less is the shield simply compared to the mast of a flagship (**ammiral**, a spelling current in Milton's time). Tne first comparison almost imperceptibly focuses on **spotty,** i.e. imperfect, even unnatural; and the second neatly deflates the magnificence of the first. Cf. the Introduction, above, pp. 55–6. (The simile may involve a personal recollection, always provided that Milton looked through a telescope during his visit to Italy.)

296   marl soil

298   vaulted with fire The flames rose to form a vaulting overhead.
299   Nath'less nevertheless
302-4   Thick as autumnal leaves etc. Perhaps the most famous simile in English literature, it borrows the basic analogy from other poets (Homer, Virgil, Dante) but adds as always a dimension which looks beyond the description to the unfolding action. The reference to **Vallombrosa** (literally 'Shady Valley', a region not far from Florence) connects this simile with the previous one (284 ff.), even as the **overarch'd** shades recall the **vaulted** flames (298). The moral implications are also inescapable: the fallen angels, for all the astonishing beauty they still retain, are now cut off from the 'living strength' of God (433), and are slowly dying. Their glory will soon be described as 'wither'd' (612).

In worst extremes, and on the perilous edge
Of battle when it rag'd, in all assaults
Their surest signal, they will soon resume
New courage and revive, though now they lie
Grovelling and prostrate on yon lake of fire,   280
As we erewhile, astounded and amaz'd,
No wonder, fall'n such a pernicious highth.

   He scarce had ceas'd when the superior fiend
Was moving toward the shore; his ponderous shield
Ethereal temper, massy, large and round,   285
Behind him cast; the broad circumference
Hung on his shoulders like the moon, whose orb
Through optic glass the Tuscan artist views
At ev'ning from the top of Fesole,
Or in Valdarno, to descry new lands,   290
Rivers or mountains in her spotty globe.
His spear, to equal which the tallest pine
Hewn on Norwegian hills, to be the mast
Of some great ammiral, were but a wand,
He walk'd with to support uneasy steps   295
Over the burning marl, not like those steps
On heaven's azure, and the torrid clime
Smote on him sore besides, vaulted with fire;
Nath'less he so endur'd, till on the beach
Of that inflamed sea, he stood and call'd   300
His legions, angel forms, who lay entranc'd
Thick as autumnal leaves that strow the brooks
In Vallombrosa, where th' Etrurian shades
High overarch'd imbow'r; or scatter'd sedge
Afloat, when with fierce winds Orion arm'd   305
Hath vex'd the Red Sea coast, whose waves o'erthrew

304–13 The second part of the epic simile confirms the implications of the first. The dying angels, like the severed autumnal leaves, are now compared to the Egyptians who drowned as they pursued the Israelites (**the sojourners of Goshen**) across the Red Sea. Cf. Exodus 14. The two parts of the simile are further related through the allusion to **Busiris** (who like every Pharaoh was regarded as a type of Satan), the reference to the storms usually associated with the constellation **Orion** (here a 'natural' instrument of Divine Justice), and the precise **sedge** or seaweed (304) which relates to the thickly-scattered leaves (302). The entire simile finally focuses on the decisive words **Abject and lost** (312). '**Abject**' means 'cast down' (the Latin *abjectus*); and '**lost**' recalls the reiterated theme of loss (cf. 85), now reinterpreted as a divine judgement.

313 **amazement** stupefaction

Busiris and his Memphian chivalry,
While with perfidious hatred they pursu'd
The sojourners of Goshen, who beheld
From the safe shore their floating carcasses   310
And broken chariot wheels, so thick bestrewn
Abject and lost lay these, covering the flood,
Under amazement of their hideous change.
He call'd so loud, that all the hollow deep
Of hell resounded. Princes, potentates,   315
Warriors, the flow'r of heav'n, once yours, now lost,
If such astonishment as this can seize
Eternal spirits; or have ye chos'n this place
After the toil of battle to repose
Your wearied virtue, for the ease you find   320
To slumber here, as in the vales of heav'n?
Or in this abject posture have ye sworn
T' adore the conqueror? who now beholds
Cherub and seraph rolling in the flood
With scatter'd arms and ensigns, till anon   325
His swift pursuers from heav'n gates discern
Th' advantage, and descending tread us down
Thus drooping, or with linked thunderbolts
Transfix us to the bottom of this gulf.
Awake, arise, or be for ever fall'n.   330
    They heard, and were abash'd, and up they sprung
Upon the wing, as when men wont to watch
On duty, sleeping found by whom they dread,
Rouse and bestir themselves ere well awake.
Nor did they not perceive the evil plight   335
In which they were, or the fierce pains not feel;
Yet to their general's voice they soon obey'd

338–43 The organic relationship of Milton's similes deserves special attention. Here the incident described in Exodus 10.12–15, where Moses (**Amram's son**) called down on the Egyptians the plague of locusts, is directly related to the destruction of the Pharaoh's army (304 ff.). The **potent rod** (338) here serves the same function as the reference to **Orion arm'd** did before (305). But now the ever-increasing deflation of the fallen angels becomes particularly emphatic as Satan's grandiose disciples are likened to deadly locusts

341   warping floating, but cf. also 'warped'

345   cope canopy, roof

348   great sultan The frequency with which Milton associates hell with tyrannous Oriental states reaches here one of its high peaks. The process will culminate in the opening lines of Book II.

351–5 Heralded by the reference to the **great sultan** (348), this simile carries the full burden of Milton's denunciation of hell's barbarism, as represented by the invading armies of Huns, Goths, and Vandals, who crossed the boundaries of the Roman Empire on the Rhine and the Danube, and thence spread to North Africa (**the Lybian sands**).

364–75 Milton accepts the traditional belief that the fallen angels became in time the gods of the heathen world. Cf. Romans 1.23: '[Men] changed the glory of the uncorruptible God into an image made like to corruptible man, and to birds, and fourfooted beasts, and creeping things'.

Innumerable. As when the potent rod
Of Amram's son in Egypt's evil day
Wav'd round the coast, up call'd a pitchy cloud   340
Of locusts, warping on the eastern wind,
That o'er the realm of impious Pharaoh hung
Like night, and darken'd all the land of Nile:
So numberless were those bad angels seen
Hovering on wing under the cope of hell   345
'Twixt upper, nether, and surrounding fires;
Till, as a signal giv'n, th' uplifted spear
Of their great sultan waving to direct
Their course, in even balance down they light
On the firm brimstone, and fill all the plain;   350
A multitude, like which the populous north
Pour'd never from her frozen loins, to pass
Rhene or the Danaw, when her barbarous sons
Came like a deluge on the south, and spread
Beneath Gibraltar to the Lybian sands.   355
Forthwith from every squadron and each band
The heads and leaders thither haste where stood
Their great commander; godlike shapes and forms
Excelling human, princely dignities,
And powers that erst in heaven sat on thrones;   360
Though of their names in heav'nly records now
Be no memorial blotted out and raz'd
By their rebellion, from the books of life.
Nor had they yet among the sons of Eve
Got them new names, till wand'ring o'er the earth,   365
Through God's high sufferance for the trial of man,
By falsities and lies the greatest part
Of mankind they corrupted to forsake

376 ff. Milton pauses to invoke the Muse once more as he prepares to embark on one of the great conventions of epic poetry—his list of pagan deities (392–522), analogous to the catalogues of ships in Homer (*The Iliad*, II, 484 ff.) and warriors in Virgil (*The Aeneid* VII, 641 ff.).

386–7 thron'd etc. In Psalm 80.1 God is addressed as 'thou that dwellest between the cherubims'.

389 Abominations the usual Biblical word for idolatrous worship

391 affront confront

392 Moloch Molech (literally 'king'), an Ammonite sun-god who was appeased by human sacrifices. See note on 400–1.

397–9 Rabba the Ammonite capital **Argob** a place in the region of **Basan** near the river **Arnon.** The barbarism of hell (above, note on 351–5) is now also intimated through the harsh names listed hereafter.

God their creator, and th' invisible
Glory of him that made them, to transform   370
Oft to the image of a brute, adorn'd
With gay religions full of pomp and gold,
And devils to adore for deities:
Then were they known to men by various names,
And various idols through the heathen world.   375
Say, Muse, their names then known, who first, who last,
Rous'd from their slumber, on that fiery couch,
At their great emperor's call, as next in worth
Came singly where he stood on the bare strand,
While the promiscuous crowd stood yet aloof?   380
The chief were those who from the pit of hell
Roaming to seek their prey on earth, durst fix
Their seats long after next the seat of God,
Their altars by his altar, gods ador'd
Among the nations round, and durst abide   385
Jehovah thund'ring out of Sion, thron'd
Between the cherubim; yea, often plac'd
Within his sanctuary itself their shrines,
Abominations; and with cursed things
His holy rites, and solemn feasts profan'd,   390
And with their darkness durst affront his light.
First Moloch, horrid king besmear'd with blood
Of human sacrifice, and parents' tears,
Though for the noise of drums and timbrels loud
Their children's cries unheard, that passed through fire 395
To his grim idol. Him the Ammonite
Worshipp'd in Rabba and her wat'ry plain,
In Argob and in Basan, to the stream
Of utmost Arnon. Nor content with such

400–1 the wisest heart/Of Solomon Solomon was swayed by his pagan wives to order the construction of 'an high place for Chemosh, the abomination of Moab, in the hill that is before Jerusalem, and for Molech, the abomination of the children of Ammon' (I Kings 11.7). The pagan temples were built on the Mount of Olives (**that opprobrious hill**, 403).

404–5 Hinnom was a deep valley near Jerusalem; the site of idolatrous worship, it became a type of hell (**Tophet**). **Gehenna** is a Greek form of the Hebrew *Ghe-hinnom*, 'Valley of Hinnom'.

406 Chemos Chemosh, a Moabite sun-god. See note on 400–1.

407–13 Aroar, Mount (?) **Nebo**, the **Abarim** hills, **Hesebon** (Heshbon), **Heronaim, Sibma Eleale**(h), the **Asphaltic Pool** (i.e. the Dead Sea, called *lacus asphaltites* because of the bitumen floating on its surface), and **Sittim**: Moabite places mentioned in Numbers 32, Isaiah 15–16, etc. **Peor** is Baal-Peor, the foremost god of the Canaanites.

416 that hill of scandal the 'opprobrious hill' of 403

417 lust hard by hate Increasingly, we observe, Milton associates violent passions with sexual perversion; the tendency will culminate in the revelation of the relationships within the 'infernal Trinity' of Satan, Sin and Death (see note on II, 790 ff.).

418 Josiah cleansed Jerusalem of its heathen temples (2 Kings 23.13)

422 Baalim and Ashtaroth A preliminary glance at the cluster of gods to be listed later in detail (437 ff.). The two names are the plural forms of the sun-god Baal and the moon-goddess Ashtoreth, the aggregate of the idols worshipped under different forms within the area bounded by the rivers Euphrates on the east and Besor (the **brook** of 420) on the Egyptian frontier to the south. The spelling of **Ashtaroth** is rather unique with Milton, who normally avoids the 'sh' sound: cf. Chemos, not Chemosh; Hesebon, not Heshbon; etc.

423–31 A summary statement of the nature of angelic beings, preparatory to the change in the size of the fallen angels in 777–80.

Audacious neighbourhood, the wisest heart   400
Of Solomon he led by fraud to build
His temple right against the temple of God
On that opprobrious hill, and made his grove
The pleasant valley of Hinnom, Tophet thence
And black Gehenna call'd, the type of hell.   405
Next Chemos, th' obscene dread of Moab's sons,
From Aroar to Nebo, and the wild
Of southmost Abarim; in Hesebon
And Horonaim, Seon's realm, beyond
The flow'ry dale of Sibma clad with vines.   410
And Eleale to th' Asphaltic Pool.
Peor his other name, when he entic'd
Israel in Sittim on their march from Nile
To do him wanton rites, which cost them woe.
Yet thence his lustful orgies he enlarg'd   415
Ev'n to that hill of scandal, by the grove
Of Moloch homicide, lust hard by hate;
Till good Josiah drove them thence to hell.
With these came they, who from the bord'ring flood
Of old Euphrates to the brook that parts   420
Egypt from Syrian ground, had general names
Of Baalim and Ashtaroth, those male,
These feminine. For spirits when they please
Can either sex assume, or both; so soft
And uncompounded is their essence pure,   425
Not tied or manacl'd with joint or limb,
Nor founded on the brittle strength of bones,
Like cumbrous flesh; but in what shape they choose
Dilated or condens'd, bright or obscure,
Can execute their airy purposes,   430

435   bestial in the form of beasts; but also 'obscene'

438–41   Astoreth the singular of Ashtaroth (422), the **Sidonian** (i.e. Phoenician) moon goddess equivalent to Venus.

443–4   th' offensive mountain, built/By that uxorious king Solomon's 'opprobrious hill' (see note on 400–1). Within the larger context of the poem, Solomon's behaviour anticipates Adam's subservience to Eve.

446   Thammuz a Syrian god equivalent to Adonis, the lover of Astoreth/ Venus (438). Slain by a boar but permitted to return to life once a year, Thammuz was worshipped in frenzied rites when the river in Lebanon bearing his name would run red (the result of the red clay brought down by spring torrents). Cf. the Introduction, above, p. 57.

455   Ezekiel saw 'Then he brought me to the door of the gate of the Lord's house (cf. 'the sacred porch' of 454) . . . and behold, there sat women weeping for Tammuz' (Ezekiel 8.14).

457   Judah the people of Israel, here **alienated** from God

457–66   Dagon (462) the Philistine god whose image was maimed when it fell before the Ark of the Covenant (I Samuel 5.4). **Azotus** (Ashdod), **Gath, Ascalon, Accaron** (Ekron), **Gaza**: the five cities of the Philistines

460   groundsill threshold

And works of love or enmity fulfil.
For these the race of Israel oft forsook
Their living strength, and unfrequented left
His righteous altar, bowing lowly down
To bestial gods; for which their heads as low   435
Bow'd down in battle, sunk before the spear
Of despicable foes. With these in troop
Came Astoreth, whom the Phoenicians call'd
Astarte, queen of heav'n, with crescent horns;
To whose bright image nightly by the moon   440
Sidonian virgins paid their vows and songs,
In Sion also not unsung, where stood
Her temple on th' offensive mountain, built
By that uxorious king, whose heart though large,
Beguil'd by fair idolatresses, fell   445
To idols foul. Thammuz came next behind,
Whose annual wound in Lebanon allur'd
The Syrian damsels to lament his fate
In amorous ditties all a summer's day,
While smooth Adonis from his native rock   450
Ran purple to the sea, suppos'd with blood
Of Thammuz yearly wounded: the love-tale
Infected Sion's daughters with like heat,
Whose wanton passions in the sacred porch
Ezekiel saw, when by the vision led   455
His eye survey'd the dark idolatries
Of alienated Judah. Next came one
Who mourn'd in earnest, when the captive Ark
Maim'd his brute image, head and hands lopp'd off
In his own temple, on the groundsill edge,   460
Where he fell flat, and sham'd his worshippers:

467–76 Rimmon a Syrian god worshipped in Damascus; his idol was duplicated by King **Ahaz** for sacrifices in Jerusalem (2 Kings 16.10–15). But while Rimmon gained a convert in Ahaz, he lost another in the leprous Syrian general Naaman (2 Kings 5.17–19).

478 The sun-god **Osiris,** his wife **Isis** and their son **Orus** (Horus) were Egyptian deities represented in animal guises. According to the legend related in Ovid's *Metamorphoses* V, 319–31, these deities were the Olympian gods fleeing—**wand'ring** (481)—from their war with the Giants (cf. above, 197–208).

484 The calf in Oreb (or Horeb, as in 7): the Israelites, during Moses' absence on Mount Sinai, fashioned a calf from the gold they had **borrow'd** from the Egyptians (Exodus 12.35–6, 32.2–4).

484–9 the rebel king Jeroboam—the rebel against Rehoboam, Solomon's successor—set up two calves of gold (**Doubl'd that sin,** 485). These **bleating gods** are contemptuously dismissed in the light of God's actual authority, as demonstrated in the slaying of the Egyptians' first-born children and cattle. (Cf. 1 Kings 12.28–9, Exodus 12.12.)

490 Belial came last, 'timorous and slothful' (II, 117): not any single deity but a vice personified; hence the difference in his presentation here (cf. Mammon, below, 678)

Dagon his name, sea monster, upward man
And downward fish: yet had his temple high
Rear'd in Azotus, dreaded through the coast
Of Palestine, in Gath and Ascalon   465
And Accaron and Gaza's frontier bounds.
Him follow'd Rimmon, whose delightful seat
Was fair Damascus, on the fertile banks
Of Abbana and Pharphar, lucid streams.
He also against the house of God was bold: 470
A leper once he lost and gain'd a king,
Ahaz his sottish conqueror, whom he drew
God's altar to disparage and displace
For one of Syrian mode, whereon to burn
His odious off'rings, and adore the gods   475
Whom he had vanquish'd. After these appear'd
A crew who under names of old renown,
Osiris, Isis, Orus and their train
With monstrous shapes and sorceries abus'd
Fanatic Egypt and her priests, to seek   480
Their wand'ring gods disguis'd in brutish forms
Rather than human. Nor did Israel scape
Th' infection when their borrow'd gold compos'd
The calf in Oreb: and the rebel king
Doubl'd that sin in Bethel and in Dan,   485
Lik'ning his maker to the grazed ox,
Jehovah, who in one night when he pass'd
From Egypt marching, equal'd with one stroke
Both her first born and all her bleating gods.
Belial came last, than whom a spirit more lewd   490
Fell not from heaven, or more gross to love
Vice for itself: to him no temple stood

495 Ely's sons Cf. I Samuel 2.12: 'Now the sons of Eli were the sons of Belial; they knew not the Lord.'

502 flown swollen

503 Sodom See Genesis 19.4–11.

504 Gibeah See Judges 19.

508–21 Th' Ionian gods were held to be the descendants of **Javan** the son of Japheth the son of Noah (Genesis 10.2), yet also to have been born later than their parents Uranus (**Heaven**) and Ge (**Earth**)—a manifest absurdity. The religious centres of Greece enumerated here include Mount **Ida** in Crete, where Zeus (Jupiter) was born; Mount **Olympus**, the seat of the foremost gods; and the oracles of Apollo at **Delphi** and of Zeus at **Dodona** in Epirus. For the myths involving Saturn's rebellion, see note on 197–208; Saturn was finally banished by his son Jupiter and fled across the Adriatic (**Adria**) to Italy **th' Hesperian fields**), France (**the Celtic**), and the British Isles (**the utmost isles**).

516 the middle air the second of the three regions into which the air was divided, the domain of the fallen angels after the fall of man

523 damp depressed

Or altar smok'd; yet who more oft than he
In temples and at altars, when the priest
Turns atheist, as did Ely's sons, who fill'd   495
With lust and violence the house of God.
In courts and palaces he also reigns
And in luxurious cities, where the noise
Of riot ascends above their loftiest tow'rs,
And injury and outrage: and when night   500
Darkens the streets, then wander forth the sons
Of Belial, flown with insolence and wine.
Witness the streets of Sodom, and that night
In Gibeah, when th' hospitable door
Expos'd a matron to avoid worse rape.   505
These were the prime in order and in might;
The rest were long to tell, though far renown'd,
Th' Ionian gods, of Javan's issue held
Gods, yet confess'd later than Heav'n and Earth
Their boasted parents; Titan heav'n's first born   510
With this enormous brood, and birthright seiz'd
By younger Saturn, he from mightier Jove
His own and Rhea's son like measure found;
So Jove usurping reign'd: these first in Crete
And Ida known, thence on the snowy top   515
Of cold Olympus rul'd the middle air
Their highest heav'n; or on the Delphian cliff,
Or in Dodona, and through all the bounds
Of Doric land; or who with Saturn old
Fled over Adria to th' Hesperian fields,   520
And o'er the Celtic roam'd the utmost isles.
All these and more came flocking; but with looks
Downcast and damp, yet such wherein appear'd

528   recollecting 're-collecting', i.e. recovering

531   warlike the common denominator of the sounds produced in hell.
The incongruity is often made absurd in the extreme, as in the juxtaposition
of the music from 'soft pipes' (561) and the horrendous 'shout that tore hell's
concave' (542).

534   Azazel a 'prince of the devils' according to the apocryphal Book of
Enoch (10.4)

537   meteor comet, usually thought to portend evil. Cf. Shakespeare,
I Henry VI, I, i, 2 ff.; *King John*, III, iv, 153 ff.; *Julius Caesar*, II, ii, 30 f.
542   concave roof
543   Chaos and old Night See below, II, 890 ff.
546   orient bright, resplendent. The excessive splendour of the occasion
carries its own moral judgement.
547   helms helmets
548   serried locked together
551   phalanx a square battle formation (cf. 758). **Dorian mood** a mode of
Greek music, sometimes commended as appropriate to martial endeavours.
551–3   such as rais'd etc. Milton's association of the activities of the fallen
angels with the commonly accepted norm of 'heroism' becomes most apparent
in the Archangel Michael's subsequent attack on the world's 'heroes':

> For in those days might only shall be admir'd,
> And valour and heroic virtue call'd;
> To overcome in battle, and subdue
> Nations, and bring home spoils with infinite
> Manslaughter, shall be held the highest pitch
> Of human glory, and for glory done
> Of triumph, to be styl'd great conquerors,
> Patrons of mankind, gods, and sons of gods,
> Destroyers rightlier call'd and plagues of men.
> Thus fame shall be achiev'd, renown on earth,
> And what most merits fame in silence hid.
>
>   (XI, 689–99)

Obscure some glimpse of joy, to have found their chief
Not in despair, to have found themselves not lost   525
In loss itself; which on his count'nance cast
Like doubtful hue: but he his wonted pride
Soon recollecting, with high words, that bore
Semblance of worth, not substance, gently rais'd
Their fainting courage, and dispell'd their fears.   530
Then straight commands that at the warlike sound
Of trumpets loud and clarions be uprear'd
His mighty standard; that proud honour claim'd
Azazel as his right, a cherub tall:
Who forthwith from the glittering staff unfurl'd   535
Th' imperial ensign, which full high advanc'd
Shone like a meteor streaming to the wind
With gems and golden lustre rich imblaz'd,
Seraphic arms and trophies: all the while
Sonorous metal blowing martial sounds: 540
At which the universal host upsent
A shout that tore hell's concave, and beyond
Frighted the reign of Chaos and old Night.
All in a moment through the gloom were seen
Ten thousand banners rise into the air   545
With orient colours waving: with them rose
A forest huge of spears: and thronging helms
Appear'd, and serried shields in thick array
Of depth immeasurable: anon they move
In perfect phalanx to the Dorian mood   *formation & music.* 550
Of flutes and soft recorders; such as rais'd
To highth of noblest temper heroes old
Arming to battle, and instead of rage
Deliberate valour breath'd, firm and unmov'd

556 swage assuage

563 horrid bristling(with spears)

568 traverse across

573 since created man since man was created (the Latin construction *post hominem creatum*)
574 embodied merged into one body
575 small infantry the Pygmies 'that pygmean race', 780), thought to engage in battle annually with migrating cranes (*The Iliad* III, 1–5)
576–87 The armies which in comparison to Satan's are mere Pygmies, include the participants in the great cycles of heroic warfare—Greek (576–9), British (579-81), and French and Italian (582–7). The Greek cycle involves the wars at **Thebes** and Troy (**Ilium**); the British: the exploits of King Arthur (**Uther's son**); and the French and Italian: the encounters between Christians and Moslems. Milton is selecting ruthlessly from the mass of available material which, inconsistent as it often was, leads him to claim that Charlemagne fell at **Fontarabbia**; but only the rearguard was massacred, some forty miles away, at Roncesvalles. Poetically, at any rate, the passage is one of the most brilliant in the poem.
576 Phlegra the site of the war of the Giants(cf. note on 197–208)
581 Armoric from Brittany(Armorica)

With dread of death to flight or foul retreat,   555
Nor wanting power to mitigate and swage
With solemn touches, troubl'd thoughts, and chase
Anguish and doubt and fear and sorrow and pain
From mortal or immortal minds. Thus they
Breathing united force with fixed thought   560
Mov'd on in silence to soft pipes that charm'd
Their painful steps o'er the burnt soil; and now
Advanc'd in view they stand, a horrid front
Of dreadful length and dazzling arms, in guise
Of warriors old with order'd spear and shield,   565
Awaiting what command their mighty chief
Had to impose: he through the armed files
Darts his experienc'd eye, and soon traverse
The whole battalion views, their order due,
Their visages and stature as of gods,   570
Their number last he sums. And now his heart
Distends with pride, and hard'ning in his strength
Glories: for never since created man,
Met such embodied force, as nam'd with these
Could merit more than that small infantry   575
Warr'd on by cranes: though all the giant brood
Of Phlegra with th' heroic race were join'd
That fought at Thebes and Ilium, on each side
Mix'd with auxiliar gods; and what resounds
In fable or romance of Uther's son   580
Begirt with British and Armoric knights;
And all who since, baptis'd or infidel
Jousted in Aspramont or Montalban,
Damasco, or Marocco, or Trebisond,
Or whom Biserta sent from Afric shore   585

588   observ'd obeyed (the Latin *observare*, to attend to)

592   her i.e. form (the Latin *forma* is feminine)

593–7 Satan's excess of glory is being steadily reduced—precisely as the sun's can be, either through mist (594–6) or through an eclipse (596–9). Eclipses, like comets (cf. 537), were thought to portend evil; but in this instance the portent is **disastrous** (literally 'ill-starred', 597) not only to man but to Satan himself—who later falls like an eclipse (XI, 181–4).

603   considerate conscious

609   amerc'd punished by being deprived of

612   wither'd cf. note on 302–4

615   blasted withered by the lightning

When Charlemain with all his peerage fell
By Fontarabbia. Thus far these beyond
Compare of mortal prowess, yet observ'd
Their dread commander: he above the rest
In shape and gesture proudly eminent   590
Stood like a tow'r; his form had yet not lost
All her original brightness, nor appear'd
Less than archangel ruin'd, and th' excess
Of glory obscur'd: as when the sun new ris'n
Looks through the horizontal misty air   595
Shorn of his beams, or from behind the moon
In dim eclipse disastrous twilight sheds
On half the nations, and with fear of change
Perplexes monarchs. Dark'n'd so, yet shone
Above them all th' archangel: but his face   600
Deep scars of thunder had intrench'd, and care
Sat on his faded cheek, but under brows
Of dauntless courage, and considerate pride
Waiting revenge: cruel his eye, but cast
Signs of remorse and passion to behold   605
The fellows of his crime, the followers rather
(Far other once beheld in bliss) condemn'd
For ever now to have their lot in pain,
Millions of spirits for his fault amerc'd
Of heav'n, and from eternal splendours flung   610
For his revolt, yet faithful how they stood,
Their glory wither'd. As when heaven's fire
Hath scath'd the forest oaks, or mountain pines,
With singed top their stately growth though bare
Stands on the blasted heath. He now prepar'd   615
To speak; whereat their doubl'd ranks they bend

620   Tears etc. Nowhere else in Books I-II is Satan closer to a tragic character than here. His behaviour argues that his heart has not yet been hardened totally—however suspect his every gesture may appear to be by this point.

624   event outcome (the Latin *eventus*)

633   emptied heav'n a manifest exaggeration. Tradition—on the authority of Revelation 12.4—had fixed the number of Satan's followers at one third of all the angels (as Raphael affirms later in the poem, V, 710).

636   different differing (?)

642   tempted our attempt Punning of this sort ('paranomasia') was much admired by Renaissance rhetoricians.

646   close secret

From wing to wing, and half enclose him round
With all his peers: attention held them mute.
Thrice he assay'd, and thrice in spite of scorn, *passion*
Tears such as angels weep, burst forth: at last   620
Words interwove with sighs found out their way.

   O myriads of immortal spirits, O powers
Matchless, but with th' almighty, and that strife
Was not inglorious, though th' event was dire,
As this place testifies, and this dire change   625
Hateful to utter: but what power of mind
Foreseeing or presaging, from the depth
Of knowledge past or present, could have fear'd,
How such united force of gods, how such
As stood like these, could ever know repulse?   630
For who can yet believe, though after loss,
That all these puissant legions, whose exile
Hath emptied heav'n, shall fail to re-ascend
Self-rais'd, and repossess their native seat?
For me be witness all the host of heav'n,   635
If counsels different, or danger shunn'd
By me, have lost our hopes. But he who reigns
Monarch in heav'n, till then as one secure
Sat on his throne, upheld by old repute,
Consent or custom, and his regal state   640
Put forth at full, but still his strength conceal'd,
Which tempted our attempt, and wrought our fall.
Henceforth his might we know, and know our own
So as not either to provoke, or dread
New war, provok'd; our better part remains   645
To work in close design, by fraud or guile
What force effected not: that he no less

651 fame rumour (the Latin *fama*). This is the 'prophesy or report' specified in the Argument of Book I.

668 Clash'd etc. recalls the custom of Roman soldiers who applauded by clashing their weapons to their shields

670-5 Mining was often regarded by Renaissance poets—no less than by Ovid, *Metamorphoses* I, 125–42—as symbolic of tampering with the natural order: see especially 685–8, below. Milton also agreed in his account of Satan's mining during the war in heaven (VI, 507–15), and here reinforces the perverse activity by his juxtaposition of 'his' and 'womb'.

674 sulphur thought to be one of the two base metals; the other was mercury

678 Mammon like Belial (490), a vice personified—in this instance avarice (from the Biblical word for 'riches', Matthew 6.24)

At length from us may find, who overcomes
By force, hath overcome but half his foe.
Space may produce new worlds; whereof so rife   650
There went a fame in heav'n that he ere long
Intended to create, and therein plant
A generation, whom his choice regard
Should favour equal to the sons of heav'n:
Thither, if but to pry, shall be perhaps   655
Our first eruption, thither or elsewhere:
For this infernal pit shall never hold
Celestial spirits in bondage, nor th' abyss
Long under darkness cover. But these thoughts
Full counsel must mature: peace is despaired,   660
For who can think submission? War then, war
Open or understood must be resolv'd.

   He spake: and to confirm his words, outflew
Millions of flaming swords, drawn from the thighs
Of mighty cherubim; the sudden blaze   665
Far round illumin'd hell: highly they rag'd
Against the highest, and fierce with grasped arms
Clash'd on their sounding shields the din of war,
Hurling defiance toward the vault of heav'n.

   There stood a hill not far whose grisly top   670
Belch'd fire and rolling smoke; the rest entire
Shone with a glossy scurf, undoubted sign
That in his womb was hid metallic ore,
The work of sulphur. Thither wing'd with speed
A numerous brigade hasten'd. As when bands   675
Of pioneers with spade and pickaxe arm'd
Forerun the royal camp, to trench a field,
Or cast a rampart. Mammon led them on,

P.L. 1/2—E

682 gold as claimed by Revelation 21.21

684 vision beatific the scholastic term for the 'happy-making sight' of God (as Milton translates it in his poem 'On Time', 18).

688 treasures better hid cf. Horace's 'aurum irrepertum et sic melius situm' (*Od.*, III, iii, 49).
689 wound The unnatural wound here is later contrasted to the productive wound on Adam's side which brought forth Eve (VIII, 465–8).
690 admire wonder
692 precious bane an oxymoron, whereby the adjective contradicts the noun

694 Babel the Tower of Babel (Gen. 11 4–9) **the works of Memphian** (Egyptian) **kings** the Pyramids

702 Sluic'd led by sluices
703 founded the massy ore etc. melted the ore in various cells, and scummed off the worthless matter (**dross**) which rose from the boiling ore (**bullion**)

Mammon, the least erected spirit that fell
From heav'n, for ev'n in heav'n his looks and thoughts   680
Were always downward bent, admiring more
The riches of heav'n's pavement, trodd'n gold,
Than aught divine or holy else enjoy'd
In vision beatific: by him first
Men also, and by his suggestion taught,   685
Ransack'd the centre, and with impious hands
Rifl'd the bowels of their mother earth
For treasures better hid. Soon had his crew
Op'n'd into the hill a spacious wound
And digg'd out ribs of gold. Let none admire   690
That riches grow in hell; that soil may best   _Catholic?_
Deserve the precious bane. And here let those
Who boast in mortal things, and wondering tell
Of Babel, and the works of Memphian kings
Learn how their greatest monuments of fame,   695
And strength and art are easily outdone
By spirits reprobate, and in an hour
What in an age they with incessant toil
And hands innumerable scarce perform.
Nigh on the plain in many cells prepar'd,   700
That underneath had veins of liquid fire
Sluic'd from the lake, a second multitude
With wondrous art founded the massy ore,   _double word — influences our_
Severing each kind, and scumm'd the bullion dross: _attitude to it._
A third as soon had form'd within the ground   705
A various mould, and from the boiling cells
By strange conveyance fill'd each hollow nook,   _like ice cube_
As in an organ from one blast of wind   _tray_
To many a row of pipes the sound-board breathes.

710 ff. Pandemonium (literally 'the home of all the demons') is modelled on classical structures. But its nominal affinities with classical architecture should not blind us to Milton's important qualifications. The reference to the **exhalation** (711) is sufficient warning, for it carries the same ominous implications as 'meteor' (537) and 'eclipse' (597). The golden roof of Pandemonium, moreover, is an inversion of the golden pavement of heaven (682); while the superimposition of the gilt entablature on severe Doric columns argues vulgarity—in itself reinforced by the magnificence of the Orient, as before (notes on 351-5, 397-9). See further the Introduction, above, p. 60 ff.
713-16 pilasters set in the walls are here said to be surrounded by Doric columns which support the entablature. The latter consists of a beam (**architrave**) and a horizontal band of sculpture (**frieze**) embossed in relief (**bossy**) and surmounted by the **cornice**.
717   Babylon was celebrated for its iniquity.
718 Alcairo Memphis (modern Cairo)
720 Belus Bel, the Babylonian Baal **Serapis** an Egyptian deity of the lower world.

728 cressets 'iron baskets of burning fragments of the bitumen, or *asphalt*, from which the *naphtha* was extracted' (Hughes). Cf. 'Asphaltic Pool' (411).
730 As from a sky The attempts of the fallen angels to imitate the glories of heaven are at best pathetic, at worst sinister. That they stand 'admiring the structure is a judgement on their distorted values.

737 Each in his hierarchy Milton, like the majority of his Protestant contemporaries, rejected the traditional arrangement of angels into nine precisely-named orders grouped in three hierarchies; but the idea of order which the arrangement implied was maintained just the same.
739 Ausonian land Italy
740 Mulciber (or Vulcan)-Hephaestus, the Greek god of metal-workers, had been expelled from heaven by Zeus (*The Iliad*, I, 591 ff.). The uncompromising comment in 747 (**Erring**) should be placed within context of Milton's consistent attempts to maintain the superiority of the Christian faith over Graeco-Roman mythology.

Anon out of the earth a fabric huge   710
Rose like an exhalation, with the sound
Of dulcet symphonies and voices sweet,
Built like a temple, where pilasters round
Were set, and Doric pillars overlaid
With golden architrave; nor did there want   715
Cornice or frieze, with bossy sculptures grav'n,
The roof was fretted gold. Not Babylon,
Nor great Alcairo such magnificence
Equall'd in all their glories, to enshrine
Belus or Serapis their gods, or seat   720
Their kings, when Egypt with Assyria strove
In wealth and luxury. Th' ascending pile
Stood fix'd her stately highth, and straight the doors
Op'ning their brazen folds discover wide
Within, her ample spaces, o'er the smooth   725
And level pavement: from the arched roof
Pendant by subtle magic many a row
Of starry lamps and blazing cressets fed
With naptha and asphaltus yielded light
As from a sky. The hasty multitude   730
Admiring enter'd, and the work some praise
And some the architect: his hand was known
In heav'n by many a tow'red structure high,
Where sceptred angels held their residence,
And sat as princes, whom the supreme king   735
Exalted to such power, and gave to rule,
Each in his hierarchy, the orders bright.
Nor was his name unheard or unador'd
In ancient Greece; and in Ausonian land
Men call'd him Mulciber; and how he fell   740

758 squared cf. *phalanx* (550)

765 paynim heathen, especially Saracen. Cf. the wars recited above, 582 ff.

768–75 Milton's simile is again based on celebrated antecedents (*The Iliad* II, 87–90; *The Aeneid* I, 430–6).
769 Taurus the constellation of the Bull, the second sign of the Zodiac, is entered by the sun in April.

From heav'n, they fabl'd, thrown by angry Jove
Sheer o'er the crystal battlements: from morn
To noon he fell, from noon to dewy eve,
A summer's day; and with the setting sun
Dropp'd from the zenith like a falling star,   745
On Lemnos th' Aegean isle: thus they relate,
Erring; for he with this rebellious rout
Fell long before; nor aught avail'd him now
To have built in heav'n high tow'rs; nor did he scape
By all his engines, but was headlong sent   750
With his industrious crew to build in hell.
Meanwhile the winged heralds by command
Of sov'reign power, with awful ceremony
And trumpets' sound throughout the host proclaim
A solemn council forthwith to be held   755
At Pandemonium, the high capital
Of Satan and his peers: their summons call'd
From every band and squared regiment
By place or choice the worthiest; they anon
With hundreds and with thousands trooping came   760
Attended: all access was throng'd, the gates
And porches wide, but chief the spacious hall
(Though like a cover'd field, where champions bold
Wont ride in arm'd and at the soldan's chair
Defied the best of paynim chivalry   765
To mortal combat or career with lance)
Thick swarm'd, both on the ground and in the air,
Brush'd with the hiss of rustling wings. As bees
In spring time, when the sun with Taurus rides,
Pour forth their populous youth about the hive   770
In clusters; they among fresh dews and flowers

774   expatiate walk abroad

777 ff.   See note on 423–31.

778   giant sons See note on 197 ff.

780   pygmean race the 'small infantry' of 575. The process of Milton's deflation of the fallen angels continues apace: the juxtaposition of 'great seraphic lords and cherubim' (794) and 'smallest forms' (789) speaks for itself.

781   the Indian mount the Himalayas. The pygmies were often said to live in India.

791   Though without number still Though they were still innumerable

795   close secret (as in 646). Note also the distinctly ecclesiastical term **conclave** (cf. 'Synod' in II, 391).

797   Frequent crowded

798   consult consultation. See the commentary in the Introduction, above, p. 61 ff.

Fly to and fro, or on the smoothed plank,
The suburb of their straw-built citadel,
New rubbed with balm, expatiate and confer
Their state affairs. So thick the airy crowd   775
Swarm'd and were strait'n'd; till the signal giv'n.
Behold a wonder! they but now who seem'd
In bigness to surpass earth's giant sons
Now less than smallest dwarfs, in narrow room
Throng numberless, like that pygmean race   780
Beyond the Indian mount, or faery elves,
Whose midnight revels, by a forest side
Or fountain some belated peasant sees,
Or dreams he sees, while overhead the moon
Sits arbitress, and nearer to the earth   785
Wheels her pale course, they on their mirth and dance
Intent, with jocund music charm his ear;
At once with joy and fear his heart rebounds.
Thus incorporeal spirits to smallest forms
Reduc'd their shapes immense, and were at large,   790
Though without number still amidst the hall
Of that infernal court. But far within
And in their own dimensions like themselves
The great seraphic lords and cherubim
In close recess and secret conclave sat   795
A thousand demi-gods on golden seats,
Frequent and full. After short silence then
And summons read, the great consult began.

AWE.

The Argument of Book II

The consulation begun, Satan debates whether another battle be to be hazarded for the recovery of heaven: some advise it, others dissuade: a third proposal is preferred, mentioned before by Satan, to search the truth of that prophecy or tradition in heaven concerning another world, and another kind of creature equal or not much inferior to themselves, about this time to be created: their doubt who shall be sent on this difficult search: Satan their chief undertakes alone the voyage, is honoured and applauded. The council thus ended, the rest betake them several ways and to several employments, as their inclinations lead them, to entertain the time till Satan return. He passes on his journey to Hell Gates, finds them shut, and who sat there to guard them, by whom at length they are opened, and discover to him the great gulf between hell and heaven; with what difficulty he passes through, directed by Chaos, the power of that place, to the sight of this new world which he sought.

1–4 The cumulative witness of Book I to the barbarism and vulgarity of
Hell is explicitly merged here with the idea of Satan as an Oriental despot
(cf. his description as 'sultan' in I, 348). The lines also forewarn us that the forth-
coming debate will only appear to be 'democratic', in line with Milton's
earlier insistence on 'Semblance of worth, not substance' (I, 529).

2 Ormus an island in the Persian Gulf, the centre of the trade in pearls with
Ind(ia)

5 by merit Satan's 'sense of injur'd merit' (I, 98) is now dismissed by
Milton with savage mockery.

9 Vain war Milton's derisive mockery links with the 'vain attempt' of I, 44.
success outcome (as in 123, below)

21 merit Satan's interpretation of the term has already been undermined by
Milton (5).

28 thunderer Associating God with Jupiter, Satan endeavours to convey an impression of a tyrannous deity.

32 none sure etc. See note on 471–3, below.

39 prosper . . prosperity a play on words; cf. I, 642

41 open war or covert guile the limits of the debate which Satan imposes (as before, I, 121 and 661–2) and which Beëlzebub will enforce later (below, 310 ff.)
43 Moloch The violence and crudity of his speech follows the pattern suggested in I, 392 ff. Cf. the commentary in the Introduction, above, p. 63.

51 sentence opinion (the Latin *sententia*)
52 unexpert inexperienced

Foremost to stand against the thunderer's aim
Your bulwark, and condemns to greatest share
Of endless pain? Where there is then no good   30
For which to strive, no strife can grow up there
From faction; for none sure will claim in hell
Precedence, none, whose portion is so small
Of present pain, that with ambitious mind
Will covet more. With this advantage then   35
To union, and firm faith, and firm accord,
More than can be in heav'n, we now return
To claim our just inheritance of old,
Surer to prosper than prosperity
Could have assur'd us; and by what best way,   40
Whether of open war or covert guile,
We now debate; who can advise, may speak.
     He ceas'd, and next him Moloch, sceptred king
Stood up, the strongest and the fiercest spirit
That fought in heav'n; now fiercer by despair: 45
His trust was with th' eternal to be deem'd
Equal in strength, and rather than be less
Car'd not to be at all; with that care lost
Went all his fear: of God, or hell, or worse
He reck'd not, and these words thereafter spake.   50
     My sentence is for open war: of wiles,
More unexpert, I boast not: them let those
Contrive who need, or when they need, not now.
For while they sit contriving, shall the rest,
Millions that stand in arms, and longing wait   55
The signal to ascend, sit ling'ring here
Heav'n's fugitives, and for their dwelling place
Accept this dark opprobrious den of shame,

The prison of his tyranny who reigns
By our delay? No, let us rather choose   60
Arm'd with hell flames and fury all at once
O'er heav'n's high tow'rs to force resistless way,
Turning our tortures into horrid arms
Against the torturer; when to meet the noise
Of his almighty engine he shall hear   65
Infernal thunder, and for lightning see
Black fire and horror shot with equal rage
Among his angels; and his throne itself
Mix'd with Tartarean sulphur, and strange fire,
His own invented torments. But perhaps   70
The way seems difficult and steep to scale
With upright wing against a higher foe.
Let such bethink them, if the sleepy drench
Of that forgetful lake benumb not still,
That in our proper motion we ascend   75
Up to our native seat: descent and fall
To us is adverse. Who but felt of late
When the fierce foe hung on our brok'n rear
Insulting, and pursu'd us through the deep,
With what compulsion and laborious flight   80
We sunk thus low? Th' ascent is easy then;
Th' event is fear'd; should we again provoke
Our stronger, some worse way his wrath may find
To our destruction: if there be in hell
Fear to be worse destroy'd: what can be worse   85
Than to dwell here, driv'n out from bliss, condemn'd
In this abhorred deep to utter woe;
Where pain of unextinguishable fire
Must exercise us without hope of end

90 vassals slaves

97 this essential our (angelic) essence

99 if Moloch is less certain than Satan (I, 117) that their substance is imperishable.
100 we are at worst etc. we are as badly off as we can be short of being annihilated
101 proof experience

104 fatal established by fate—as Satan argued earlier (I, 116). But the word also means 'destructive'.

106 denounc'd displayed

109 Belial See I, 490 ff. Milton's tone now alters to suggest the 'persuasive' speech of the suave Belial. Cf. the commentary in the Introduction, above, pp. 63–4.
110 A fairer person etc. Belial was traditionally said to be 'a beautiful angel'; but he only 'seemed' etc. Cf. 'Semblance of worth, not substance' (I, 529).

114 reason argument (as in 121, below)

The vassals of his anger, when the scourge   90
Inexorably, and the torturing hour
Calls us to penance? More destroy'd than thus
We should be quite abolish'd and expire.
What fear we then? what doubt we to incense
His utmost ire? which to the highth enrag'd,   95
Will either quite consume us, and reduce
To nothing this essential, happier far
Than miserable to have eternal being:
Or if our substance be indeed divine,
And cannot cease to be, we are at worst   100
On this side nothing; and by proof we feel
Our power sufficient to disturb his heav'n,
And with perpetual inroads to alarm,
Though inaccessible, his fatal throne:
Which if not victory is yet revenge.   105
   He ended frowning, and his look denounc'd
Desperate revenge, and battle dangerous
To less then gods. On th' other side up rose
Belial, in act more graceful and humane;
A fairer person lost not heav'n; he seem'd   110
For dignity compos'd and high exploit:
But all was false and hollow; though his tongue
Dropp'd manna, and could make the worse appear
The better reason, to perplex and dash
Maturest counsels: for his thoughts were low;   115
To vice industrious, but to nobler deeds
Timorous and slothful: yet he pleas'd the ear,
And with persuasive accent thus began.
   I should be much for open war, O peers,
As not behind in hate; if what was urg'd   120

123 success outcome (as in 9, above)
124 fact feat (the Latin *factum*)

127 scope target (the Greek *skopos*).

130 watch a collective noun; hence the plural verb 'render'
131 the bordering deep the border of Chaos (described below, 1034 ff.)
132 obscure scanned 'óbscure'

139 mould substance, nature

143 flat absolute

146–54 Belial, even more decisively than Moloch (99), doubts that their angelic substance is indeed imperishable, as Satan had claimed (I, 117).

150 uncreated See 894, below.

Main reason to persuade immediate war,
Did not dissuade me most, and seem to cast
Ominous conjecture on the whole success:
When he who most excels in fact of arms,
In what he counsels and in what excels   125
Mistrustful, grounds his courage on despair
And utter dissolution, as the scope
Of all his aim, after some dire revenge.
First, what revenge? The tow'rs of heav'n are fill'd
With armed watch, that render all access   130
Impregnable; oft on the bordering deep
Encamp their legions, or with obscure wing
Scout far and wide into the realm of night,
Scorning surprise. Or could we break our way
By force, and at our heels all hell should rise   135
With blackest insurrection, to confound
Heav'n's purest light, yet our great enemy
All incorruptible would on his throne
Sit unpolluted, and th' ethereal mould
Incapable of stain would soon expel   140
Her mischief, and purge off the baser fire
Victorious. Thus repuls'd, our final hope
Is flat despair: we must exasperate
Th' almighty victor to spend all his rage,
And that must end us, that must be our cure,   145
To be no more; sad cure; for who would lose,
Though full of pain, this intellectual being,
Those thoughts that wander through eternity,
To perish rather, swallow'd up and lost
In the wide womb of uncreated night,   150
Devoid of sense and motion? And who knows,

156   Belike no doubt

165   amain with utmost speed
166   afflicting striking down; cf. I, 186

174   red right hand The reference is to the thunderbolt, the 'red lightning'
of I, 175. Cf. Jupiter's *rubens dextera*, in Horace, *Od.*, I, ii, 2.
175   Her i.e., hell's

181–2   the sport and prey etc. Cf. Virgil's 'rapidis ludibria ventis', in the
The Aeneid VI, 74–5; and *Measure for Measure* III, i, 124–6:

> To be imprison'd in the viewless winds,
> And blown with restless violence round about
> The pendent world.

Let this be good, whether our angry foe
Can give it, or will ever? How he can
Is doubtful; that he never will is sure.
Will he, so wise, let loose at once his ire,   155
Belike through impotence, or unaware,
To give his enemies their wish, and end
Them in his anger, whom his anger saves
To punish endless? Wherefore cease we then?
Say they who counsel war, we are decreed,   160
Reserv'd and destin'd to eternal woe;
Whatever doing, what can we suffer more,
What can we suffer worse? Is this then worst,
Thus sitting, thus consulting, thus in arms?
What when we fled amain, pursu'd and struck   165
With heav'n's afflicting thunder, and besought
The deep to shelter us? This hell then seem'd
A refuge from those wounds: or when we lay
Chain'd on the burning lake? That sure was worse.
What if the breath that kindl'd those grim fires   170
Awak'd should blow them into sevenfold rage
And plunge us in the flames? or from above
Should intermitted vengeance arm again
His red right hand to plague us? what if all
Her stores were open'd, and this firmament   175
Of hell should spout her cataracts of fire,
Impendent horrors, threat'ning hideous fall
One day upon our heads; while we perhaps
Designing or exhorting glorious war,
Caught in a fiery tempest shall be hurl'd   180
Each on his rock transfix'd, the sport and prey
Of racking whirlwinds, or for ever sunk

184 converse live together

187 open or conceal'd Belial is rejecting Satan's proposals (I, 661; II, 41).

191 derides cf. Psalm 2.4: 'He that sitteth in the heavens shall laugh: the Lord shall have them in derision'.

197 fate inevitable In opposition to Satan (I, 117), Belial equates fate with the will of God, even as he accepts God's omniscience (189–91) and omnipotence (192–3).

207 ignominy cf. I, 115

210 supreme scanned 'súpreme'

Under yon boiling ocean, wrapp'd in chains;
There to converse with everlasting groans,
Unrespited, unpitied, unrepriev'd,   185
Ages of hopeless end; this would be worse.
War therefore, open or conceal'd, alike
My voice dissuades; for what can force or guile
With him, or who deceive his mind, whose eye
Views all things at one view? He from heav'n's highth   190
All these our motions vain, sees and derides;
Not more almighty to resist our might
Than wise to frustrate all our plots and wiles.
Shall we then live thus vile, the race of heav'n
Thus trampl'd, thus expell'd to suffer here   195
Chains and these torments? Better these than worse
By my advice; since fate inevitable
Subdues us, and omnipotent decree,
The victor's will. To suffer, as to do,
Our strength is equal, nor the law unjust   200
That so ordains: this was at first resolv'd,
If we were wise, against so great a foe
Contending, and so doubtful what might fall.
I laugh, when those who at the spear are bold
And vent'rous, if that fail them, shrink and fear   205
What yet they know must follow, to endure
Exile, or ignominy, or bonds, or pain,
The sentence of their conqueror: this is now
Our doom; which if we can sustain and bear,
Our supreme foe in time may much remit   210
His anger, and perhaps thus far remov'd
Not mind us not offending, satisfi'd
With what is punish'd; whence these raging fires

220–1 light . . . flight one of the few rhymes in *Paradise Lost*

228 Mammon In line with the earlier delineation of his character (I, 678–84), Mammon now extends Belial's suggestion (217–19) in a direction which the latter—'timorous and slothful'—would hardly endorse. Cf. the commentary in the Introduction, above, pp. 64–5.

232 everlasting fate In agreement with Belial's equation of 'fate inevitable with the will of God (197), Mammon argues that the displacement of fate (= providence) by chance would lead to the supremacy of chaos (cf. 907 ff., below).

234–5 The former i.e., the dethronement of God **the latter** i.e., the recovery of heaven

236 supreme scanned regularly (not as in 210)

240–9 Mammon's partisan view of heaven is preparatory to his concept of independence ('Live to ourselves', 254) which Milton throughout condemns.

243 hallelujahs songs of praise (from the Hebrew phrase, 'Praise ye Jah', i.e. Jehovah)

244 envied cf. I, 35

Will slack'n, if his breath stir not their flames.
Our purer essence then will overcome   215
Their noxious vapour, or enur'd not feel,
Or chang'd at length, and to the place conform'd
In temper and in nature, will receive
Familiar the fierce heat, and void of pain;
This horror will grow mild, this darkness light,   220
Besides what hope the never-ending flight
Of future days may bring, what chance, what change
Worth waiting, since our present lot appears
For happy though but ill, for ill not worst,
If we procure not to ourselves more woe.   225
    Thus Belial with words cloth'd in reason's garb
Counsell'd ignoble ease, and peaceful sloth,
Not peace: and after him thus Mammon spake.
    Either to disenthrone the king of heav'n
We war, if war be best, or to regain   230
Our own right lost: him to unthrone we then
May hope, when everlasting fate shall yield
To fickle chance, and Chaos judge the strife:
The former vain to hope argues as vain
The latter: for what place can be for us   235
Within heav'n's bound, unless heav'n's lord supreme
We overpower? Suppose he should relent
And publish grace to all, on promise made
Of new subjection; with what eyes could we
Stand in his presence humble, and receive   240
Strict laws impos'd, to celebrate his throne
With warbl'd hymns, and to his Godhead sing
Forc'd hallelujahs; while he lordly sits
Our envied sov'reign, and his altar breathes

245 ambrosial fragrant; immortal

249 pursue try to obtain(i.e. the 'state' of 251–2)

252 vassalage cf. 'vassals' (90)

256 Hard liberty . . . easy yoke These oxymorons appear to endorse
Milton's passionate defence of individual liberty against usurping tyrants.
But within the context of the poem, Mammon's plea for liberty is shown to be
misplaced in so far as tyranny is a dimension of experience not in heaven
but in hell. The plea is also a brilliant instance of Miltonic irony, for it is
uttered by the foremost materialist among the devils.

271 Wants not does not lack
273 Magnificence such as that of Pandemonium, erected under Mam-
mon's supervision (I, 678 ff.)
275 elements The four 'elements' (fire, air, water, earth) were supposed to
have been inhabited by demonic powers. Cf. Satan's address to his disciples
in *Paradise Regained* II, 121–4:

> Princes, heav'n's ancient sons, ethereal thrones,
> Demonian spirits now, from the element
> Each of his reign allotted, rightlier call'd,   .
> Powers of fire, air, water, and earth beneath.

Ambrosial odours and ambrosial flowers,   245
Our servile offerings. This must be our task
In heav'n, this our delight; how wearisome
Eternity so spent in worship paid
To whom we hate. Let us not then pursue
By force impossible, by leave obtain'd   250
Unacceptable, though in heav'n, our state
Of splendid vassalage, but rather seek
Our own good from ourselves, and from our own
Live to ourselves, though in this vast recess,
Free, and to none accountable, preferring   255
Hard liberty before the easy yoke
Of servile pomp. Our greatness will appear
Then most conspicuous, when great things of small,
Useful of hurtful, prosperous of adverse
We can create, and in what place so e'er   260
Thrive under evil, and work ease out of pain
Through labour and endurance. This deep world
Of darkness do we dread? How oft amidst
Thick clouds and dark doth heav'n's all-ruling sire
Choose to reside, his glory unobscur'd,   265
And with the majesty of darkness round
Covers his throne; from whence deep thunders roar
Must'ring their rage, and heav'n resembles hell?
As he our darkness, cannot we his light
Imitate when we please? This desert soil   270
Wants not her hidden lustre, gems and gold;
Nor want we skill or art, from whence to raise
Magnificence; and what can heav'n show more?
Our torments also may in length of time
Become our elements, these piercing fires   275

278 sensible sense

281 Compose adjust

285–90 The simile echoes in particular *The Aeneid* X, 96–9.

294 Michael (the name is here a trisyllable): the commander of the heavenly host during the war in heaven, whose two-handed sword spread havoc among Satan's disciples (VI, 250 ff., 320 ff.)

297 policy nominally 'statesmanship' but involving 'cunning' because of its frequent use to describe Machiavellian tactics **process** scanned 'procéss'.

299 Beëlzebub Cf. I, 81, and the commentary in the Introduction, above, pp. 65–6.

301 Aspect scanned 'aspéct'
302 front forehead (the Latin *fons*)

306 Atlantean Atlas, one of the Titans, was obliged to support the sky with his shoulders for having warred on the gods. The reference recalls the elaborate simile in Book I (197 ff.); it is also invested with irony insofar as the burden of Atlas was a punishment.

As soft as now severe, our temper chang'd
Into their temper; which must needs remove
The sensible of pain. All things invite
To peaceful counsels, and the settl'd state
Of order, how in safety best we may   280
Compose our present evils, with regard
Of what we are and where, dismissing quite
All thoughts of war: ye have what I advise.
   He scarce had finish'd, when such murmur fill'd
Th' assembly, as when hollow rocks retain   285
The sound of blust'ring winds, which all night long
Had rous'd the sea, now with hoarse cadence lull
Seafaring men o'erwatch'd, whose bark by chance
Or pinnace anchors in a craggy bay
After the tempest: such applause was heard   290
As Mammon ended, and his sentence pleas'd,
Advising peace: for such another field
They dreaded worse than hell: so much the fear
Of thunder and the sword of Michael
Wrought still within them; and no less desire   295
To found this nether empire, which might rise
By policy, and long process of time,
In emulation opposite to heav'n.
Which when Beëlzebub perceiv'd, than whom,
Satan except, none higher sat, with grave   300
Aspect he rose, and in his rising seem'd
A pillar of state; deep on his front engrav'n
Deliberation sat and public care;
And princely counsel in his face yet shone,
Majestic though in ruin: sage he stood   305
With Atlantean shoulders fit to bear

310 ff. Beëlzebub's speech is a persuasive tour de force. Mindful of the approbation extended by the fallen angels first to Belial and then to Mammon, he now borrows elements from their speeches and finally proposes a compromise—significantly 'first devis'd/By Satan' (379–80; cf. I, 650 ff.).

312 style formal title

324 first and last cf. Revelation 1.11: 'I am Alpha and Omega, the first and the last'.

327–8 The golden or mild rule is again contrasted to the iron form of government when Satan is told later:

> That golden sceptre which thou didst reject
> Is now an iron rod to bruise and break
> Thy disobedience.
>
> (V, 886–8)

329 What why

330 determin'd finished ('determined the issue for us')

336 to our power to the limit of our power

337 reluctance resistance

The weight of mightiest monarchies; his look
Drew audience and attention still as night
Or summer's noon-tide air, while thus he spake.
   Thrones and imperial powers, offspring of heav'n,			310
Ethereal virtues; or these titles now
Must we renounce, and changing style be call'd
Princes of hell? For so the popular vote
Inclines, here to continue, and build up here
A growing empire; doubtless; while we dream,				315
And know not that the king of heav'n hath doom'd
This place our dungeon, not our safe retreat
Beyond his potent arm, to live exempt
From heav'n's high jurisdiction, in new league
Banded against his throne, but to remain				320
In strictest bondage, though thus far remov'd,
Under th' inevitable curb, reserv'd
His captive multitude: for he, be sure,
In highth or depth, still first and last will reign
Sole king, and of his kingdom lose no part				325
By our revolt, but over hell extend
His empire, and with iron sceptre rule
Us here, as with his golden those in heav'n.
What sit we then projecting peace and war?
War hath determin'd us, and foil'd with loss				330
Irreparable; terms of peace yet none
Vouchsaf'd or sought; for what peace will be giv'n
To us enslav'd, but custody severe,
And stripes, and arbitrary punishment
Inflicted? and what peace can we return,				335
But to our power hostility and hate,
Untam'd reluctance, and revenge though slow,

P.L. 1/2—F

346   fame See note on I, 650.

350   favour'd more Cf. Psalm 8.5: 'Thou hast made [man] a little lower than the angels, and hast crowned him with glory and honour'.
352   oath The episode has parallels in both the Old Testament (Genesis 22.16, Isaiah 13.12–13, Hebrews 12.26, etc.) and epic poetry (*The Iliad*, I, 530, and *The Aeneid* IX, 106).

356   endu'd gifted
357   attempted assailed

366   drive expel
367   puny weak; also 'born later' ('born since us', the French legal term *puis né*)

Yet ever plotting how the conqueror least
May reap his conquest, and may least rejoice
In doing what we most in suffering feel?   340
Nor will occasion want, nor shall we need
With dangerous expedition to invade
Heav'n, whose high walls fear no assault or siege,
Or ambush from the deep. What if we find
Some easier enterprise? There is a place   345
(If ancient and prophetic fame in heav'n
Err not) another world, the happy seat
Of some new race call'd Man, about this time
To be created like to us, though less
In power and excellence, but favour'd more   350
Of him who rules above; so was his will
Pronounc'd among the gods, and by an oath,
That shook heav'n's whole circumference, confirm'd.
Thither let us bend all our thoughts, to learn
What creatures there inhabit, of what mould,   355
Or substance, how endu'd, and what their power,
And where their weakness, how attempted best,
By force or subtlety: though heav'n be shut,
And heav'n's high arbitrator sit secure
In his own strength, this place may lie expos'd   360
The utmost border of his kingdom, left
To their defence who hold it: here perhaps
Some advantageous act may be achiev'd
By sudden onset, either with hell fire
To waste his whole creation, or possess   365
All as our own, and drive as we were driv'n,
The puny habitants, or if not drive,
Seduce them to our party, that their God

375 **originals** parentage

376 **Advise** consider

379–80 **first devis'd/By Satan** See I, 650 ff.

383 **one root** Adam and Eve, the root of the human family tree

387 **states** orders; cf. 'Estates of the Realm'

391 **Synod** cf. the ecclesiastical term 'conclave' in I, 795

May prove their foe, and with repenting hand
Abolish his own works. This would surpass   370
Common revenge, and interrupt his joy
In our confusion, and our joy upraise
In his disturbance; when his darling sons
Hurl'd headlong to partake with us, shall curse
Their frail originals, and faded bliss,   375
Faded so soon. Advise if this be worth
Attempting, or to sit in darkness here
Hatching vain empires. Thus Beëlzebub
Pleaded his devilish counsel, first devis'd
By Satan, and in part propos'd: for whence,   380
But from the author of all ill could spring
So deep a malice, to confound the race
Of mankind in one root, and earth with hell
To mingle and involve, done all to spite
The great creator? But their spite still serves   385
His glory to augment. The bold design
Pleas'd highly those infernal states, and joy
Sparkl'd in all their eyes; with full assent
They vote: whereat his speech he thus renews.
    Well have ye judg'd, well ended long debate,   390
Synod of gods, and like to what ye are,
Great things resolv'd, which from the lowest deep
Will once more lift us up, in spite of fate,
Nearer our ancient seat; perhaps in view
Of those bright confines, whence with neighbouring arms 395
And opportune excursion we may chance
Re-enter heav'n; or else in some mild zone
Dwell not unvisited of heav'n's fair light
Secure, and at the bright'ning orient beam

404   tempt attempt

405   unbottom'd bottomless, the Greek word for *abyss* (ἄβυσσος); but cf. the 'bottomless pit' of Revelation 20.3

406   palpable obscure Cf. the 'darkness which may be felt', one of the plagues of Egypt (Exodus 10.21)

407   uncouth unknown

409   abrupt abyss—the realm of Chaos   **arrive** arrive at

410   The happy isle The created universe floats in space like an island in the midst of the ocean of Chaos. Cf. below p. 213.

412   stations posts

415   suffrage election

418   suspense in suspense

420   all sat mute In a parallel episode in Book III (217 ff.), God the Father calls for a volunteer to save man and the Son of God offers himself meekly, in striking contrast to Satan's 'monarchal pride' here.

Purge off this gloom; the soft delicious air,   400
To heal the scar of these corrosive fires
Shall breathe her balm. But first whom shall we send
In search of this new world, whom shall we find
Sufficient? Who shall tempt with wand'ring feet
The dark unbottom'd infinite abyss   405
And through the palpable obscure find out
His uncouth way, or spread his airy flight
Upborne with indefatigable wings
Over the vast abrupt, ere he arrive
The happy isle; what strength, what art can then   410
Suffice, or what evasion bear him safe
Through the strict sentries and stations thick
Of angels watching round? Here he had need
All circumspection, and we now no less
Choice in our suffrage; for on whom we send,   415
The weight of all and our last hope relies.
    This said, he sat; and expectation held
His look suspense, awaiting who appear'd
To second, or oppose, or undertake
The perilous attempt: but all sat mute,   420
Pondering the danger with deep thoughts; and each
In other's count'nance read his own dismay
Astonish'd: none among the choice and prime
Of those heav'n-warring champions could be found
So hardy as to proffer or accept   425
Alone the dreadful voyage; till at last
Satan, whom now transcendent glory rais'd
Above his fellows, with monarchal pride
Conscious of highest worth, unmov'd thus spake.
    O progeny of heav'n, empyreal thrones,   430

432 long is the way etc. cf. Virgil, *The Aeneid* IV, 126–9, and Dante, *Inferno* XXXIX, 95
434 convex of fire the vault of hell, here seen as it were from outside (else it would be *concave*, as in 635, below)

438 profound a noun

439 unessential having no substance or being; mere 'vacuity' (below, 932)

441 abortive monstrous, 'lifeless'

443 remains awaits

448 moment importance

452 Refusing if I refuse

457 intend consider

461 deceive beguile

With reason hath deep silence and demur
Seiz'd us, though undismay'd: long is the way
And hard, that out of hell leads up to light;
Our prison strong, this huge convex of fire,
Outrageous to devour, immures us round   435
Ninefold, and gates of burning adamant
Barr'd over us prohibit all egress.
These pass'd, if any pass, the void profound
Of unessential night receives him next
Wide gaping, and with utter loss of being   440
Threatens him, plung'd in that abortive gulf.
If thence he scape into whatever world,
Or unknown region, what remains him less
Than unknown dangers and as hard escape.
But I should ill become this throne, O peers,   445
And this imperial sov'reignty, adorn'd
With splendour, arm'd with power, if aught propos'd
And judg'd of public moment, in the shape
Of difficulty or danger could deter
Me from attempting. Wherefore do I assume   450
These royalties, and not refuse to reign,
Refusing to accept as great a share
Of hazard as of honour, due alike
To him who reigns, and so much to him due
Of hazard more, as he above the rest   455
High honour'd sits? Go therefore mighty powers,
Terror of heav'n, though fall'n; intend at home,
While here shall be our home, what best may ease
The present misery, and render hell
More tolerable; if there be cure or charm   460
To respite or deceive, or slack the pain

467 prevented anticipated, forestalled; possibly even 'hindered'
468 rais'd encouraged

471–3 The resolution here stands in marked contrast to Satan's earlier claim that 'none sure will claim in hell/Precedence, none' (II, 32–3).

478 awful full of awe or reverence **prone** grovelling, unlike the 'lowly reverent' angels in heaven (III, 349)—or indeed man before the fall, 'erect and tall,/God-like erect' (IV, 288–9)

485 close secret (as in I, 795)

488–95 another sustained simile, again related to the previous one (285–90), and here marking the devils' change of mood
490 element sky

492 If chance if it chances that

Of this ill mansion: intermit no watch
Against a wakeful foe, while I abroad
Through all the coasts of dark destruction seek
Deliverance for us all: this enterprise   465
None shall partake with me. Thus saying rose
The monarch, and prevented all reply,
Prudent, lest from his resolution rais'd
Others among the chief might offer now
(Certain to be refus'd) what erst they fear'd;   470
And so refus'd might in opinion stand
His rivals, winning cheap the high repute
Which he through hazard huge must earn. But they
Dreaded not more th' adventure than his voice
Forbidding; and at once with him they rose;   475
Their rising all at once was as the sound
Of thunder heard remote. Towards him they bend
With awful reverence prone; and as a god
Extol him equal to the highest in heav'n:
Nor fail'd they to express how much they prais'd,   480
That for the general safety he despis'd
His own: for neither do the spirits damn'd
Lose all their virtue; lest bad men should boast
Their specious deeds on earth, which glory excites,
Or close ambition varnish'd o'er with zeal.   485
Thus they their doubtful consultations dark
Ended rejoicing in their matchless chief:
As when from mountain tops the dusky clouds
Ascending, while the north wind sleeps, o'erspread
Heav'n's cheerful face, the louring element   490
Scowls o'er the dark'n'd landscape snow, or show'r;
If chance the radiant sun with farewell sweet

496-505 A decisive denunciation of war, not unlike several other irenic statements in the poem (cf. note on I, 550-3). The context is of course pointedly ironic.

503 accord agree
504 enow enough

506 Stygian cf. I, 239

508 Midst an adverb **paramount** chief

511 god-like imitated state An explicit statement of tendencies repeatedly noted by Milton earlier; cf. V, 763: 'Affecting equality with God'.
512 globe compact band
513 emblazonry heraldic devices **horrent** (the same as 'horrid', cf. II, 63) bristling
514 ff. As only 'the great seraphic lords and cherubim' had attended the proceedings (I, 794), the result must now be proclaimed to their followers.
516 the four winds the four quarters of the compass
517 alchemy brass

522 ranged assembled in ranks

Extend his ev'ning beam, the fields revive,
The birds their notes renew, and bleating herds
Attest their joy, that hill and valley rings.   495
O shame to men! Devil with devil damn'd
Firm concord holds, men only disagree
Of creatures rational, though under hope
Of heav'nly grace: and God proclaiming peace,
Yet live in hatred, enmity, and strife   500
Among themselves, and levy cruel wars,
Wasting the earth, each other to destroy:
As if (which might induce us to accord)
Man had not hellish foes enow besides,
That day and night for his destruction wait.   505
   The Stygian council thus dissolv'd; and forth
In order came the grand infernal peers,
Midst came their mighty paramount, and seem'd
Alone th' antagonist of heav'n, nor less
Then hell's dread emperor with pomp supreme,   510
And god-like imitated state; him round
A globe of fiery seraphim enclos'd
With bright emblazonry, and horrent arms.
Then of their session ended they bid cry
With trumpets regal sound the great result: 515
Toward the four winds four speedy cherubim
Put to their mouths the sounding alchemy
By herald's voice explain'd: the hollow abyss
Heard far and wide, and all the host of hell
With deaf'ning shout, return'd them loud acclaim.   520
Thence more at ease their minds and somewhat rais'd
By false presumptuous hope, the ranged powers
Disband, and wand'ring, each his several way

526 entertain while away

528–46 The account of the fallen angels' 'games' is indebted to *The Iliad* II, 773 ff., and *The Aeneid* V, 577 ff., and especially VI, 640 ff. Here as elsewhere, however, the 'heroic' occasion is undermined through sinister implications (533–7) and, more obviously still, violence (539–41).

528 sublime uplifted

530 th' Olympian games were the most important festival of ancient Greece; other games included the **Pythian,** held at Delphi in honour of Apollo.

531 goal the turning post in the Roman arena around which chariots were swung.

532 fronted opposed

538 welkin sky

539 Typhoean cf. note on I, 197 ff

542–6 Alcides (Hercules), returning from **Oechalia** where he had killed Eurytus, put on a poisoned robe sent by his wife Deianira. **Lichas** who had brought the robe was thrown by the maddened Hercules from the top of Mount **Oeta** in Thessaly into the **Euboic** (Euboean) Sea.

552 partial prejudiced, i.e. in favour of themselves **harmony** cf. note on I, 531

554 Suspended held rapt **took** enchanted

Pursues, as inclination or sad choice
Leads him perplex'd, where he may likeliest find   525
Truce to his restless thoughts, and entertain
The irksome hours, till his great chief return.
Part on the plain, or in the air sublime
Upon the wing, or in swift race contend,
As at th' Olympian games, or Pythian fields;   530
Part curb their fiery steeds, or shun the goal
With rapid wheels, or fronted brigades form.
As when to warn proud cities war appears
Wag'd in the troubl'd sky, and armies rush
To battle in the clouds, before each van   535
Prick forth the airy knights, and couch their spears
Till thickest legions close; with feats of arms
From either end of heav'n the welkin burns.
Others with vast Typhoean rage more fell
Rend up both rocks and hills, and ride the air   540
In whirlwind; hell scarce holds the wild uproar.
As when Alcides from Oechalia crown'd
With conquest, felt th' envenom'd robe, and tore
Through pain up by the roots Thessalian pines,
And Lichas from the top of Oeta threw   545
Into th' Euboic sea. Others more mild,
Retreated in a silent valley, sing
With notes angelical to many a harp
Their own heroic deeds and hapless fall
By doom of battle; and complain that fate   550
Free virtue should enthral to force or chance.
Their song was partial, but the harmony
(What could it less when spirits immortal sing?)
Suspended hell, and took with ravishment

561 found no end the gradual decay of the fallen angels is both physical (above, note on I, 302–4) and, as emphasized here, intellectual. The **Vain wisdom** of the Stoics denounced in 564–9 is similarly held to be inadequate in the light of the ·Christian ideals upheld in *Paradise Lost.*

568–9 Cf. Horace, *Od.*, II, iii, 9: 'illi robur et aes triplex/circa pectus erat'.
568 obdured hardened
569 stubborn patience is later contrasted to the true patience finally acknowledged by Adam (XII, 553 ff.)
570 gross compact
571 wide far and wide
572 clime region

575–81 The **four infernal rivers** often mentioned by other poets (e.g. Virgil in *The Aeneid* VI, 265, 295, etc.) are here precisely characterised: **Styx** is **hate; Acheron, sorrow; Cocytus, lamentation;** and **Phlegethon, fire.** Similarly **Lethe** (583) derives from the Greek word meaning a forgetting.

583 Lethe similar to, but not the same as, the 'forgetful lake of' II, 74

The thronging audience. In discourse more sweet   555
(For eloquence the soul, song charms the sense,)
Others apart sat on a hill retir'd,
In thoughts more elevate, and reason'd high
Of providence, foreknowledge, will and fate,
Fix'd fate, free will, foreknowledge absolute,   560
And found no end, in wand'ring mazes lost.
Of good and evil much they argu'd then,
Of happiness and final misery,
Passion and apathy, and glory and shame,
Vain wisdom all, and false philosophy: 565
Yet with a pleasing sorcery could charm
Pain for a while or anguish, and excite
Fallacious hope, or arm th' obdured breast
With stubborn patience as with triple steel.
Another part in squadrons and gross bands,   570
On bold adventure to discover wide
That dismal world, if any clime perhaps
Might yield them easier habitation, bend
Four ways their flying march, along the banks
Of four infernal rivers that disgorge   575
Into the burning lake their baleful streams;
Abhorred Styx the flood of deadly hate,
Sad Acheron of sorrow, black and deep;
Cocytus, nam'd of lamentation loud
Heard on the rueful stream; fierce Phlegethon   580
Whose waves of torrent fire inflame with rage.
Far off from these a slow and silent stream,
Lethe the river of oblivion rolls
Her wat'ry labyrinth, whereof who drinks,
Forthwith, his former state and being forgets,   585

592 Serbonian bog Lake Serbonis, on the coast of Lower Egypt between **Damiata** (modern Damietta) and **Mount Casius,** was said to have been sufficiently treacherous to devour 'whole armies'.

594 parching drying

595 frore frozen. Cf. Ecclesiasticus 43.20–21: 'When the cold north wind bloweth, . . . [it] burneth the wilderness, and consumeth the grass as fire'.

596 The Greek **Furies** (Erinyes, Eumenides) were endowed by Virgil with the claws of the Harpies (*The Aeneid* III, 211–18). Both Furies and Harpies were agents of divine vengeance. **hal'd** dragged

599 The **fierce extremes** of alternating bitter cold and excessive heat were characteristic of the classical Hades no less than of the Judaeo–Christian hell. Cf. Dante, *Inferno* XXXII, 29 ff., and Shakespeare, *Measure for Measure* III, i, 118 ff.

600 starve perish with cold

611 Medusa one of the three Gorgons or female monsters with wings, brazen claws, and hair of hissing serpents; the sight of their face would turn men to stone

614 Tantalus a mythical king whom Zeus punished by confining him to Hades where he was 'tantalised' by being placed just beyond the reach of ever-receding water (*The Odyssey* XI, 582–92)

Forgets both joy and grief, pleasure and pain.
Beyond this flood a frozen continent
Lies dark and wild, beat with perpetual storms
Of whirlwind and dire hail, which on firm land
Thaws not, but gathers heap, and ruin seems   590
Of ancient pile; all else deep snow and ice,
A gulf profound as that Serbonian bog
Betwixt Damiata and Mount Casius old,
Where armies whole have sunk: the parching air
Burns frore, and cold performs th' effect of fire.   595
Thither by harpy-footed Furies hal'd,
At certain revolutions all the damn'd
Are brought: and feel by turns the bitter change
Of fierce extremes, extremes by change more fierce,
From beds of raging fire to starve in ice   600
Their soft ethereal warmth, and there to pine
Immovable, infix'd, and frozen round,
Periods of time, thence hurried back to fire.
They ferry over this Lethean sound
Both to and fro, their sorrow to augment,   605
And wish and struggle, as they pass, to reach
The tempting stream, with one small drop to lose
In sweet forgetfulness all pain and woe,
All in one moment, and so near the brink;
But fate withstands, and to oppose th' attempt   610
Medusa with Gorgonian terror guards
The ford, and of itself the water flies
All taste of living wight, as once it fled
The lip of Tantalus. Thus roving on
In confus'd march forlorn, th' advent'rous bands   615
With shudd'ring horror pale, and eyes aghast

620 alp any high mountain

621 The dreary monotony of hell is admirably suggested by the dull thud of the monosyllables.

625 prodigious unnatural

628 On **Gorgons** see above, note on 611. The **Hydra** was a destructive serpent with nine heads; and the **Chimera,** a fire-breathing monster (*The Iliad* VI, 181).

632 Explores tests, puts to proof

635 concave roof. See above, I, 542.

636–40 The simile draws on the trading voyages to the East, here envisaged as starting from **Bengala** (Bengal), passing through **Ternate** and **Tidor** (two of the Moluccas or Spice Islands), and after crossing the **Ethiopian** Sea (the Indian Ocean), sailing round the **Cape** of Good Hope toward Europe. The simile's relevance may be studied by examining the **nightly** movement of the fleet, and the **drugs** it transports.

637 equinoctial winds the trade winds which blow at the equinoxes

642 the pole the South Pole

647 impal'd enclosed

View'd first their lamentable lot, and found
No rest: through many a dark and dreary vale
They pass'd, and many a region dolorous,
O'er many a frozen, many a fiery alp,   620
Rocks, caves, lakes, fens, bogs, dens, and shades of death,
A universe of death, which God by curse
Created evil, for evil only good,
Where all life dies, death lives, and nature breeds,
Perverse, all monstrous, all prodigious things,   625
Abominable, inutterable and worse
Than fables yet have feign'd, or fear conceiv'd,
Gorgons and Hydras, and Chimeras dire.
   Meanwhile the adversary of God and man,
Satan with thoughts inflam'd of highest design,   630
Puts on swift wings, and towards the gates of hell
Explores his solitary flight; sometimes
He scours the right hand coast, sometimes the left,
Now shaves with level wing the deep, then soars
Up to the fiery concave towering high.   635
As when far off at sea a fleet descri'd
Hangs in the clouds, by equinoctial winds
Close sailing from Bengala, or the isles
Of Ternate and Tidore, whence merchants bring
Their spicy drugs: they on the trading flood   640
Through the wide Ethiopian to the Cape
Ply stemming nightly toward the pole. So seem'd
Far off the flying fiend: at last appear
Hell bounds high reaching to the horrid roof,
And thrice threefold the gates; three folds were brass,   645
Three iron, three of adamantine rock,
Impenetrable, impal'd with circling fire,

649 ff. The celebrated allegory of Sin (650 ff.) and Death (666 ff.) is based on the Biblical affirmation that 'when lust was conceived, it bringeth forth sin: and sin, when it is finished, bringeth forth death' (James 1.15). The allegory does not intrude upon the poem abruptly; Milton has repeatedly suggested—as in the description of the great demonic powers (above, I, 490 ff., 678 ff.)—that physical details often intimate spiritual states of mind (cf. note on I, 48). The tendency is confirmed by the details provided below, especially 762 ff. See further the commentary in the Introduction, above, p. 70 ff.

650 ff. Milton's Sin has affinities with Ovid's Scylla (*Metamorphoses* XIV, 40–74), Spenser's Errour (*The Faerie Queene* I, i, 14 ff.), and other less well-known predecessors such as Phineas Fletcher's Hamartia or Sin (*The Purple Island* XII, 27–31). Thus the dogs around Sin's waist are Ovid's contribution; and her serpentine lower parts, Spenser's:

> Halfe like a serpent horribly desplaide,
> But th' other halfe did womans shape retaine.

651   scaly cf. note on I, 206

652   Voluminous rolling

653   mortal sting cf. I Corinthians 15.56: 'The sting of death is sin'

655   Cerberian mouths like the mouths of Cerberus, the three-headed dog guarding the entrance to Hades. Appropriately, Sin is also 'the portress of hell' (746).

659–61 Scylla's lower parts were transformed by Circe into a mass of yelping dogs; later, she was transformed into a rock set in the Straits of Messina between **Calabria** and **Trinacria** (Sicily).

662   night-hag any witch, but perhaps Hecate, the queen of witches, in particular; her charms were used by Circe to effect Scylla's transformation.

665   Lapland traditionally regarded as the home of witches.

665–6 Witches were popularly said to have power over the moon, often causing it to **labour** (cf. the Latin *laborare*, to be eclipsed).

666 ff. Milton increases the effectiveness of his conception of Death by leaving him alarmingly vague even as his actual presence is never in doubt. Cf. the precedent in *The Faerie Queene* VII, vii, 46:

> Death with most grim and griesly visage seen,
> Yet is he nought but parting of the breath:
> Ne ought to see, but like a shade to ween,
> Unbodied, unsoul'd, unheard, unseen.

673   crown cf: Revelation 6.2: 'a crown was given unto him [death], and he went conquering, and to conquer'

677   admir'd wondered

678   except excluded

Yet unconsum'd. Before the gates there sat
On either side a formidable shape;
The one seem'd woman to the waist, and fair,   650
But ended foul in many a scaly fold
Voluminous and vəst, a serpent arm'd
With mortal sting: about her middle round
A cry of hell hounds never ceasing bark'd
With wide Cerberian mouths full loud, and rung   655
A hideous peal: yet, when they list, would creep,
If aught disturb'd their noise, into her womb,
And kennel there, yet there still bark'd and howl'd,
Within unseen. Far less abhorr'd than these
Vex'd Scylla bathing in the sea that parts   660
Calabria from the hoarse Trinacrian shore:
Nor uglier follow the night-hag, when call'd
In secret, riding through the air she comes
Lur'd with the smell of infant blood, to dance
With Lapland witches, while the labouring moon   665
Eclipses at their charms. The other shape,
If shape it might be call'd that shape had none
Distinguishable in member, joint, or limb,
Or substance might be call'd that shadow seem'd,
For each seem'd either; black it stood as night,   670
Fierce as ten Furies, terrible as hell,
And shook a dreadful dart; what seem'd his head
The likeness of a kingly crown had on.
Satan was now at hand, and from his seat
The monster moving onward came as fast   675
With horrid strides, hell trembled as he strode.
Th' undaunted fiend what this might be admir'd,
Admir'd, not fear'd; God and his Son except,

686 proof experience

688 goblin demon, evil spirit

692 the third part See above, note on I, 633.

693 Conjur'd sworn together (the Latin *coniurare*)

701 scorpions Cf. I Kings 12.11: 'I will chastise you with scorpions'.

706 deform hideous (the Latin *deformis*)

708–11 Popular superstition considered comets to portend disaster (as above, I, 537). But the simile is particularly relevant to the context in that it places the comet in the constellation of **Ophiuchus** (Serpent Bearer), thereby anticipating Satan's later transformation into a serpent. The **horrid hair** may also glance back at the Gorgons' hair of serpent (above, 611); but it is also faithful to the original Greek word for 'comet',: κομήτης, 'long-haired'.

Created thing nought valu'd he nor shunn'd;
And with disdainful look thus first began.   680
    Whence and what art thou, execrable shape,
That dar'st, though grim and terrible, advance
Thy miscreated front athwart my way
To yonder gates? Through them I mean to pass,
That be assur'd, without leave ask'd of thee: 685
Retire, or taste thy folly, and learn by proof,
Hell-born, not to contend with spirits of heav'n.
    To whom the goblin full of wrath repli'd,
Art thou that traitor angel, art thou he,
Who first broke peace in heav'n and faith, till then   690
Unbrok'n, and in proud rebellious arms
Drew after him the third part of heav'n's sons
Conjur'd against the highest, for which both thou
And they outcast from God, are here condemn'd
To waste eternal days in woe and pain?   695
And reck'n'st thou thyself with spirits of heav'n,
Hell-doom'd, and breath'st defiance here and scorn,
Where I reign king, and to enrage thee more,
Thy king and lord? Back to thy punishment,
False fugitive, and to thy speed add wings,   700
Lest with a whip of scorpions I pursue
Thy ling'ring, or with one stroke of this dart
Strange horror seize thee, and pangs unfelt before.
    So spake the grisly terror, and in shape,
So speaking and so threat'ning, grew tenfold   705
More dreadful and deform: on th' other side
Incens'd with indignation Satan stood
Unterrifi'd, and like a comet burn'd,
That fires the length of Ophiucus huge

709–10 Ophiuchus lies in the northern hemisphere. The north, it should be noted, is traditionally associated with Satan.

716 The **Caspian** Sea was usually thought to be storm-bound.

718 mid air See note on I, 516.

721 but once i.e., when Christ would overcome both Satan and Death. Ironically, the encounter is prophesied by Sin (734).

732 ordain'd his drudge See note on I, 149–52.

In th' Arctic sky, and from his horrid hair   710
Shakes pestilence and war. Each at the head
Levell'd his deadly aim; their fatal hands
No second stroke intend, and such a frown
Each cast at th' other, as when two black clouds
With heav'n's artillery fraught, come rattling on   715
Over the Caspian, then stand front to front
Hov'ring a space, till winds the signal blow
To join their dark encounter in mid air:
So frown'd the mighty combatants, that hell
Grew darker at their frown, so match'd they stood;   720
For never but once more was either like
To meet so great a foe: and now great deeds
Had been achiev'd, whereof all hell had rung,
Had not the snaky sorceress that sat
Fast by hell gate, and kept the fatal key,   725
Ris'n, and with hideous outcry rush'd between.
    O father, what intends thy hand, she cri'd,
Against thy only son? What fury O son,
Possesses thee to bend that mortal dart
Against thy father's head? and know'st for whom;   730
For him who sits above and laughs the while
At thee ordain'd his drudge, to execute
What e'er his wrath, which he calls justice, bids,
His wrath which one day will destroy ye both.
    She spake, and at her words the hellish pest   735
Forbore, then these to her Satan return'd:
    So strange thy outcry, and thy words so strange
Thou interposest, that my sudden hand
Prevented spares to tell thee yet by deeds
What it intends; till first I know of thee,   740

746 the portress of hell gate See note on 655.

747 ff. Sin's elevated language contrasts sharply with the content of her speech, giving rise to a macabre 'comedy'. The account of her generation (752–68) may appear to be similar to the birth of Athena from the head of Zeus, but it is important to remember that the Greek myth suggests the advent of Wisdom from the Divine Mind. The birth of Sin is therefore a perversion of the birth of Athena—even as it is a gross parody of God's generation of the Son, his 'perfect image' (cf. 764). The constant efforts of the devils to imitate God (see note on 511) have presently produced the anti-Trinity of Satan, Sin and Death.

766 in secret The phrase, here as before, has evil connotations (see 663; however, in I, 6, the context drastically alters the meaning). It is also meant to stand in contrast to the 'open' consummation of the love between Adam and Eve (IV, 720 ff.).

771 the empyrean heaven (cf. I, 117)

What thing thou art, thus double-form'd, and why
In this infernal vale first met thou call'st
Me father, and that phantasm call'st my son?
I know thee not, nor ever saw till now
Sight more detestable than him and thee.   745
    To whom thus the portress of hell gate repli'd;
Hast thou forgot me then, and do I seem
Now in thine eye so foul, once deem'd so fair
In heav'n, when at th' assembly, and in sight
Of all the seraphim with thee combin'd   750
In bold conspiracy against heav'n's king,
All on a sudden miserable pain
Surpris'd thee, dim thine eyes, and dizzy swum
In darkness, while thy head flames thick and fast
Threw forth, till on the left side op'ning wide,   755
Likest to thee in shape and count'nance bright,
Then shining heav'nly fair, a goddess arm'd
Out of thy head I sprung: amazement seiz'd
All th' host of heav'n; back they recoil'd afraid
At first, and call'd me Sin, and for a sign   760
Portentous held me; but familiar grown,
I pleas'd, and with attractive graces won
The most averse, thee chiefly, who full oft
Thyself in me thy perfect image viewing
Becam'st enamour'd, and such joy thou took'st   765
With me in secret, that my womb conceiv'd
A growing burden. Meanwhile war arose,
And fields were fought in heav'n; wherein remain'd
(For what could else) to our almighty foe
Clear victory, to our part loss and rout   770
Through all the empyrean: down they fell

772 pitch height

788 Hell trembl'd Created nature is normally presented in *Paradise Lost* as reacting violently to any violation of the divine behests; here it is significant that even hell responds with horror at the birth of Death.

790 ff. Death's violation of his mother Sin, together with Satan's incestuous relationship with her, extend the sheer perversion of the demonic powers observed earlier (see note on I, 417).

795 yelling monsters on the spiritual level, the torments of conscience.

801 vex harass
802 rest or intermission cf. Isaiah 57.21: 'There is no peace, saith my God, to the wicked'.

Driv'n headlong from the pitch of heaven, down
Into this deep, and in the general fall
I also; at which time this powerful key
Into my hands was giv'n, with charge to keep   775
These gates for ever shut, which none can pass
Without my op'ning. Pensive here I sat
Alone, but long I sat not, till my womb
Pregnant by thee, and now excessive grown
Prodigious motion felt and rueful throes.   780
At last this odious offspring whom thou seest
Thine own begotten, breaking violent way
Tore through my entrails, that with fear and pain
Distorted, all my nether shape thus grew
Transform'd: but he my inbred enemy   785
Forth issu'd, brandishing his fatal dart
Made to destroy: I fled, and cry'd out Death;
Hell trembl'd at the hideous name, and sigh'd
From all her caves, and back resounded Death.
I fled, but he pursu'd (though more, it seems,   790
Inflam'd with lust than rage) and swifter far,
Me overtook his mother all dismay'd,
And in embraces forcible and foul
Ingend'ring with me, of that rape begot
These yelling monsters that with ceaseless cry   795
Surround me, as thou saw'st, hourly conceiv'd
And hourly born, with sorrow infinite
To me, for when they list into the womb
That bred them they return, and howl and gnaw
My bowels, their repast; then bursting forth   800
Afresh with conscious terrors vex me round,
That rest or intermission none I find.

809 fate Sin disagrees with Satan in equating fate with the will of God; cf. note on I, 116.

813 dint stroke

815 lore lesson

825 pretences claims

827 uncouth unknown, strange (cf. 407)

829 unfounded bottomless
830 a place foretold see above, I, 650

833 purlieus outskirts

Before mine eyes in opposition sits
Grim Death my son and foe, who sets them on,
And me his parent would full soon devour   805
For want of other prey, but that he knows
His end with mine involv'd; and knows that I
Should prove a bitter morsel, and his bane,
Whenever that shall be; so fate pronounc'd.
But thou O father, I forewarn thee, shun   810
His deadly arrow; neither vainly hope
To be invulnerable in those bright arms,
Though temper'd heav'nly, for that mortal dint,
Save he who reigns above, none can resist.
    She finish'd, and the subtle fiend his lore   815
Soon learn'd, now milder, and thus answer'd smooth.
Dear daughter, since thou claim'st me for thy sire,
And my fair son here show'st me, the dear pledge
Of dalliance had with thee in heav'n, and joys
Then sweet, now sad to mention, through dire change 820
Befall'n us unforeseen, unthought of, know
I come no enemy, but to set free
From out this dark and dismal house of pain,
Both him and thee, and all the heav'nly host
Of spirits that in our just pretences arm'd   825
Fell with us from on high: from them I go
This uncouth errand sole, and one for all
Myself expose, with lonely steps to tread
Th' unfounded deep, and through the void immense
To search with wand'ring quest a place foretold   830
Should be, and, by concurring signs, ere now
Created vast and round, a place of bliss
In the purlieus of heav'n, and therein plac'd

P.L. 1/2—G

839–44 Satan's promise is fulfilled after the fall of Man (X, 397 ff.).

842 buxom unresisting

847 famine hunger

858 Tartarus See note on 69.

A race of upstart creatures, to supply
Perhaps our vacant room, though more remov'd,   835
Lest heav'n surcharg'd with potent multitude
Might hap to move new broils: be this or aught
Than this more secret now design'd, I haste
To know, and this once known, shall soon return,
And bring ye to the place where thou and Death   840
Shall dwell at ease, and up and down unseen
Wing silently the buxom air, embalm'd
With odours; there ye shall be fed and fill'd
Immeasurably, all things shall be your prey.
He ceas'd, for both seem'd highly pleas'd, and Death   845
Grinn'd horrible a ghastly smile, to hear
His famine should be fill'd, and bless'd his maw
Destin'd to that good hour: no less rejoic'd
His mother bad, and thus bespake her sire.
    The key of this infernal pit by due,   850
And by command of heav'n's all-powerful king
I keep, by him forbidden to unlock
These adamantine gates; against all force
Death ready stands to interpose his dart,
Fearless to be o'ermatch'd by living might.   855
But what owe I to his commands above
Who hates me, and hath hither thrust me down
Into this gloom of Tartarus profound,
To sit in hateful office here confin'd,
Inhabitant of heav'n, and heav'nly-born,   860
Here in perpetual agony and pain,
With terrors and with clamours compass'd round
Of mine own brood, that on my bowels feed:
Thou art my father, thou my author, thou

868 The gods who live at ease a Homeric phrase ῥεῖα ζώοντες (*The Iliad* VI, 138; *The Odyssey* IV, 805; etc.)

869 At thy right hand This macabre ambition is an extension of the anti-Trinitanian parody noted earlier (747 ff.).

871 fatal See note on 104.

874 portcullis a heavy grating suspended by chains and sliding up and down in vertical grooves at the sides of a fortress's gateway (*Oxford English Dictionary*)

880 jarring sound Later, the opening of the 'ever-during' gates of heaven will be said to produce 'harmonious sound/On golden hinges moving' (VII, 205–7).

883 Erebus here used as a synonym for hell. Greek mythology considered Erebus to be the first child of Chaos, and Night his second—both of whom appear presently (894–5).

883–4 to shut/Excell'd her power The sin once committed, it is reserved for God to repair it.

889 redounding overflowing

890 ff. The actual state of chaos (the 'deep', as in I, 152) is on the allegorical level presided over by **Chaos,** assisted by **eldest** (cf. 'uncreated' in 150) **Night** and by **Chance** (910). But the physical details provided are later applied to the state of mind both of Satan (see the quotation in the note on I, 254–5) and the fallen Adam and Eve (Book X). Cf. the Introduction, above, pp. 52 ff., 69 ff.

My being gav'st me; whom should I obey   865
But thee, whom follow? Thou wilt bring me soon
To that new world of light and bliss, among
The gods who live at ease, where I shall reign
At thy right hand voluptuous, as beseems
Thy daughter and thy darling, without end.   870
   Thus saying, from her side the fatal key,
Sad instrument of all our woe, she took;
And towards the gate rolling her bestial train,
Forthwith the huge portcullis high updrew,
Which but herself not all the Stygian powers   875
Could once have mov'd; then in the keyhole turns
Th' intricate wards, and every bolt and bar
Of massy iron or solid rock with ease
Unfast'ns: on a sudden op'n fly
With impetuous recoil and jarring sound   880
Th' infernal doors, and on their hinges grate
Harsh thunder, that the lowest bottom shook
Of Erebus. She op'n'd, but to shut
Excell'd her power; the gates wide op'n stood,
That with extended wings a banner'd host   885
Under spread ensigns marching might pass through
With horse and chariots rank'd in loose array;
So wide they stood, and like a furnace mouth
Cast forth redounding smoke and ruddy flame.
Before their eyes in sudden view appear   890
The secrets of the hoary deep, a dark
Illimitable ocean without bound,
Without dimension, where length, breadth, and highth,
And time and place are lost; where eldest Night
And Chaos, ancestors of Nature, hold   895

898   hot, cold, moist, and dry the four elements of the created universe, here conceived as in a state of total disorder

904 The desert of **Barca** and the city of **Cyrene** were situated in North Africa between Egypt and Carthage.
905   Levied raised

911 The created universe emerged from Chaos and may (cf. 'perhaps') lapse into it again. The line is less a description of nature's actual history than a moral judgement.

919   frith 'firth' (cf. fjord), channel
920   peal'd deafened
921   ruinous crashing (cf. the Latin *rucre*, to fall)
921–2 The parenthesis translates Virgil's 'parvis componere magna solebam' (*Ecl.*, I, 24; etc.).
922   Bellona the Roman goddess of war
924   frame structure

Eternal anarchy, amidst the noise
Of endless wars, and by confusion stand.
For hot, cold, moist, and dry, four champions fierce
Strive here for mastery, and to battle bring
Their embryon atoms; they around the flag   900
Of each his faction, in their several clans,
Light-arm'd or heavy, sharp, smooth, swift or slow,
Swarm populous, unnumber'd as the sands
Of Barca or Cyrene's torrid soil,
Levied to side with warring winds, and poise   905
Their lighter wings. To whom these most adhere,
He rules a moment; Chaos umpire sits,
And by decision more embroils the fray
By which he reigns: next him high arbiter
Chance governs all. Into this wild abyss,   910
The womb of nature and perhaps her grave,
Of neither sea, nor shore, nor air, nor fire,
But all these in their pregnant causes mix'd
Confus'dly, and which thus must ever fight,
Unless th' almighty maker them ordain   915
His dark materials to create more worlds,
Into this wild abyss the wary fiend
Stood on the brink of hell and look'd a while,
Pondering his voyage; for no narrow frith
He had to cross. Nor was his ear less peal'd   920
With noises loud and ruinous (to compare
Great things with small) than when Bellona storms,
With all her battering engines bent to raze
Some capital city; or less than if this frame
Of heav'n were falling, and these elements   925
In mutiny had from her axle torn

927 vans wings

933 pennons wings (the Latin *pennae*)

937 Instinct animated—as though charged with gunpowder (**nitre**)
939 Syrtis any quicksand (from the two dangerous gulfs called Syrtes, on the coast of North Africa)
941-7 The one-eyed **Arimaspians** of Scythia were said to have coveted the gold guarded by griffins. The simile pertains to Satan's progress **half on foot,/Half flying** (941-2), in that the griffins were part lion and part eagle. On another level, Satan is again associated with unnatural monsters, as before (I, 200-1; etc.).

948-50 The avalanche of monosyllables suggests Satan's laborious—and singularly undignified—progress.

The steadfast earth. At last his sail-broad vans
He spreads for flight, and in the surging smoke
Uplifted spurns the ground, thence many a league
As in a cloudy chair ascending rides   930
Audacious, but that seat soon failing, meets
A vast vacuity: all unawares
Fluttering his pennons vain plumb down he drops
Ten thousand fathom deep, and to this hour
Down had been falling, had not by ill chance   935
The strong rebuff of some tumultuous cloud
Instinct with fire and nitre hurried him
As many miles aloft: that fury stay'd,
Quench'd in a boggy Syrtis, neither sea,
Nor good dry land: nigh founder'd on he fares,   940
Treading the crude consistence, half on foot,
Half flying; behoves him now both oar and sail.
As when a gryphon through the wilderness
With winged course o'er hill or moory dale,
Pursues the Arimaspian, who by stealth   945
Had from his wakeful custody purloin'd
The guarded gold: so eagerly the fiend
O'er bog or steep, through straight, rough, dense, or rare,
With head, hands, wings or feet pursues his way,
And swims or sinks, or wades, or creeps, or flies: 950
At length a universal hubbub wild
Of stunning sounds and voices all confus'd
Born through the hollow dark assaults his ear
With loudest vehemence: thither he plies,
Undaunted to meet there whatever power   955
Or spirit of the nethermost abyss
Might in that noise reside, of whom to ask

960–7 The personified powers are haphazardly chosen from Virgil (*The Aeneid* 268–81), Boccaccio (*Genealogy of the Gods*), Spenser (*The Faerie Queene* IV,ii, 47), *et al.* **Demogorgon** (cf. 'Gorgon' in 611) was a mysterious and therefore feared infernal deity; **Orcus** and **Ades** (Hades) are the Latin and Greek names for the lower world.

961 wasteful desolate

972 secrets secret places

977 Confine with border on (from the Latin *cum* + *finis*, a boundary)

988 anarch a word coined from 'anarchy' (cf. monarch—monarchy)

Which way the nearest coast of darkness lies
Bordering on light; when straight behold the throne
Of Chaos, and his dark pavilion spread   960
Wide on the wasteful deep; with him enthron'd
Sat sable-vested Night, eldest of things,
The consort of his reign; and by them stood
Orcus and Ades, and the dreaded name
Of Demogorgon: Rumour next and Chance,   965
And Tumult and Confusion all embroiled,
And Discord with a thousand various mouths.
     To whom Satan turning boldly, thus. Ye powers
And spirits of this nethermost abyss,
Chaos and ancient Night, I come no spy,   970
With purpose to explore or to disturb
The secrets of your realm, but by constraint
Wand'ring this darksome desert, as my way
Lies through your spacious empire up to light,
Alone, and without guide, half lost, I seek   975
What readiest path leads where your gloomy bounds
Confine with heav'n; or if some other place
From your dominion won, th' ethereal king
Possesses lately, thither to arrive
I travel this profound, direct my course;   980
Directed, no mean recompense it brings
To your behoof, if I that region lost,
All usurpation thence expell'd, reduce
To her original darkness and your sway
(Which is my present journey) and once more   985
Erect the standard there of ancient Night;
Yours be th' advantage all, mine the revenge.
     Thus Satan; and him thus the anarch old

989   incompos'd discomposed

1000   so i.e. by keeping residence

1004   heav'n the sky (but in 1006, the realm of God).
1005   golden chain See below, 1051.

1008   danger mischief

1017–18   The **Argo,** the ship of Jason and the Argonauts, was threatened during its passage through the **Bosphorus** by the Symplegades, two rocks which continually clashed together.
1019–20   Odysseus **(Ulysses)** in his passage through the Straits of Messina, avoided the monster **Charybdis** by steering to the left 'larboard' and passing closer to Scylla ('th' other whirlpool', already alluded to above, 659–61). See *The Odyssey* XII, 234 ff.

With falt'ring speech and visage incompos'd
Answer'd. I know thee, stranger, who thou art,   990
That mighty leading angel, who of late
Made head against heav'n's king, though overthrown.
I saw and heard, for such a numerous host
Fled not in silence through the frighted deep
With ruin upon ruin, rout on rout,   995
Confusion worse confounded; and heav'n gates
Pour'd out by millions her victorious bands
Pursuing. I upon my frontiers here
Keep residence; if all I can will serve,
That little which is left so to defend,   1000
Encroach'd on still through our intestine broils
Weak'ning the sceptre of old Night: first hell
Your dungeon stretching far and wide beneath;
Now lately heav'n and earth, another world
Hung o'er my realm, link'd in a golden chain   1005
To that side heav'n from whence your legions fell:
If that way be your walk, you have not far;
So much the nearer danger; go and speed;
Havoc and spoil and ruin are my gain.
    He ceas'd; and Satan stay'd not to reply,   1010
But glad that now his sea should find a shore,
With fresh alacrity and force renew'd
Springs upward like a pyramid of fire
Into the wild expanse, and through the shock
Of fighting elements, on all sides round   1015
Environ'd wins his way; harder beset
And more endanger'd, than when Argo pass'd
Through Bosphorus betwixt the jostling rocks:
Or when Ulysses on the larboard shunn'd

1021-2   The laboured rhythm suggests Satan's efforts.

1024   amain   See above, 165.

1026 ff.   The construction of the bridge linking hell with earth after the fall of Man, is more fully described later (X, 282 ff.).

1029   utmost orb   the Primum Mobile, the outermost sphere of the created universe (or **world**, 1030)

1037   nature   i.e., the created universe as opposed to the sterile domains of hell and Chaos described to this point

1048   undetermin'd square or round   infinite enough to make it impossible to determine whether it is **square** (as Revelation 21.16 suggests) or **round** (the traditional symbol of perfection)

Charybdis, and by th' other whirlpool steer'd.   1020
So he with difficulty and labour hard
Mov'd on, with difficulty and labour he;
But he once past, soon after when man fell,
Strange alteration! Sin and Death amain
Following his track, such was the will of heav'n,   1025
Pav'd after him a broad and beat'n way
Over the dark abyss, whose boiling gulf
Tamely endur'd a bridge of wondrous length
From hell continu'd reaching th' utmost orb
Of this frail world; by which the spirits perverse   1030
With easy intercourse pass to and fro
To tempt or punish mortals, except whom
God and good angels guard by special grace.
But now at last the sacred influence
Of light appears, and from the walls of heav'n   1035
Shoots far into the bosom of dim Night
A glimmering dawn; here nature first begins
Her farthest verge, and Chaos to retire
As from her outmost works a brok'n foe
With tumult less and with less hostile din,   1040
That Satan with less toil, and now with ease
Wafts on the calmer wave by dubious light
And like a weather-beaten vessel holds
Gladly the port, though shrouds and tackle torn;
Or in the emptier waste, resembling air,   1045
Weighs his spread wings, at leisure to behold
Far off th' empyreal heav'n, extended wide
In circuit, undetermin'd square or round,
With opal tow'rs and battlements adorn'd
Of living sapphire, once his native seat;   1050

1051 a golden chain was also suspended by Zeus from heaven to draw all things to himself (*The Iliad* VIII, 18–27). Variously interpreted later, it was most often held to represent (as Milton himself wrote in an academic essay) 'the universal concord and sweet union of all things which Pythagoras poetically figures as harmony'. Here it is symbolic of the connection between heaven and the created universe (**This pendent world,** 1052); later it would be replaced by the equally symbolic bridge linking the world with hell (above 1026 ff.).

And fast by hanging in a golden chain
This pendent world, in bigness as a star
Of smallest magnitude close by the moon.
Thither full fraught with mischievous revenge,
Accurs'd, and in a cursed hour he hies.   1055

Appendices

Appendices

The Universe of 'Paradise Lost'

Paradise Lost was published in 1667—well over a century after the appearance of Copernicus's revolutionary theory concerning the structure of the universe (1543), and some five decades after Galileo had provided relatively conclusive support for the Copernican thesis (1610). We naturally expect these developments to have obliged Milton to reject the older (Ptolemaic) conception of the universe which held that the sun and the planets revolve about the stationary earth, in favour of the new 'heliocentric' universe which asserted that the planets including the earth revolve about the stationary sun.

The universe of *Paradise Lost*, however, conforms to the general scheme of the obsolete theory. The earth—'the centric globe' (X, 671)—is placed firmly in the centre of the universe; the seven planets including the sun and the moon revolve around it in orbits or 'spheres' which terminate, beyond the fixed stars and the Crystalline Spheres, in the Primum Mobile—the 'utmost orb' or 'wall' of the universe (II, 1029; X, 302), an enormous 'convex' (III, 419) which encloses the entire created cosmos. Immediately outside and surrounding the 'happy isle' of the universe (II, 410) is the ever-threatening 'illimitable ocean' of Chaos (II, 892). Hell is located at the lowermost depths of Chaos, its roof a vast concave (I, 542; II, 635). Heaven —'the empyrean' (II, 771), i.e. 'made of fire'—crowns the universal structure, its position actually no less than symbolically prominent, and its form 'undetermin'd, square or round' (II, 1048).

Why does Milton's universe conform to a scientifically obsolete scheme? Partly, no doubt, because the Copernican thesis—notwithstanding Galileo's support—had not yet been endorsed in every quarter; for not only did the advocates of Ptolemaic cosmology refuse to accept the new theory but a compromise proposed by the Danish astronomer Tycho Brahe effectively prevented the unanimous endorsement of any single scheme. In *Paradise Lost* the

angel Raphael appears sufficiently well versed in scientific lore to
satisfy even the ever-curious Adam. In typical Miltonic fashion,
however, the scientific catechism is promptly placed within a more
comprehensive ethical context. Raphael asks:

> What if the sun
> Be centre to the world, and other stars
> By his attractive virtue and their own
> Incited, dance about him various rounds?

—and finally concludes:

> Solicit not thy thoughts with matters hid,
> Leave them to God above, him serve and fear.
>   (VIII, 122–68)

Raphael's conclusion will disappoint literalists in that he appears to
evade the issue. On the other hand, he reminds us forcefully that
Paradise Lost is not a scientific treatise, and that consequently the
question of Milton's use of a 'scientifically obsolete scheme' is irrele-
vant. We should rather inquire whether the universe of *Paradise
Lost* is appropriate poetically. Does it advance the poet's 'great argu-
ment'? Does it contribute substantially to his moral vision? Does it
correspond to other elements in the poem which, jointly considered,
yield an aesthetically satisfying world view?

One way to appreciate the poetic appropriateness of Milton's
'obsolete' universe is through the relationship he constantly posits
between physical details and spiritual entities. The pattern is most
obviously apparent in the deployment of the fundamental image of
fruition, gradually transformed from the literal and death-inducing
'fruit' mentioned in the opening lines of *Paradise Lost*, to the spiritual
and life-giving 'seed' which is to effect man's restoration through
Christ. Appropriately, the turning point in this transformation is
stated by the Son of God who at the outset of Book XI presents the
prayers of repentant man before the Father (my italics):

> See Father, what first *fruits* on earth are sprung
> From thy *implanted* grace in man, these sighs
> And prayers, which in this golden censer, mix'd
> With incense, I thy priest before thee bring,
> *Fruits* of more pleasing savour from thy *seed*
> Sow'n with contrition in his heart, than those
> Which his own hand manuring all the trees
> Of Paradise could have produc'd, ere fall'n
> From innocence. Now therefore bend thine ear
> To supplication, hear his sighs though mute;
> Unskilful with what words to pray, let me
> Interpret for him, me his advocate
> And propitiation, all his works on me
> Good or not good *ingraft* . . .
>
> (XI, 22–35)

In like manner the literal Chaos surrounding the 'happy isle' of our universe is related to the spiritual chaos which overwhelms Man after the fall. The domain of Chaos is first described as

> the hoary deep, a dark
> Illimitable Ocean without bound,
> Without dimension, where length, breadth, and highth,
> And time and place are lost; where eldest Night
> And Chaos, ancestors of nature, hold
> Eternal anarchy, amidst the noise
> Of endless wars, and by confusion stand.
> For hot, cold, moist, and dry, four champions fierce
> Strive here for mastery, and to battle bring
> Their embryon atoms . . .
>
> (II, 891–900)

The description looks ahead to the experiences of the fallen Adam and Eve in Book IX:

> They sat them down to weep, nor only tears
> Rain'd at their eyes, but high winds worse within
> Began to rise, high passions, anger, hate,
> Mistrust, suspicion, discord, and shook sore
> Their inward state of mind, calm region once
> And full of peace, now toss'd and turbulent:
> For understanding rul'd not, and the will
> Heard not her lore, both in subjection now
> To sensual appetite, who from beneath
> Usurping over sov'reign reason claim'd
> Superior sway . . .
>
> (IX, 1121–31)

In juxtaposition the two passages yield any number of words which are applicable to the literal details no less than to the spiritual experience: 'dark' and 'lost', 'anarchy' and 'confusion', 'fierce' and 'toss'd' and 'turbulent'. Even more important, however, is the crucial phrase 'from beneath/Usurping'. The moral judgement inherent in the phrase confirms one's persuasion that Milton's 'obsolete' universe provides a schematic outline of the great issues presented within the poem as a whole.

Yet the old-fashioned confines of the poetic universe of *Paradise Lost* are so adjusted by Milton as to accommodate at least one aspect which derives exclusively from the new astronomy. I refer to that impressive characteristic of Milton's universe which is its enormous space. At once measureless and infinite at least in appearance, the vast space of Milton's world is a testimony to his conviction that only an infinite universe can afford God opportunities to display his infinite goodness. The argument was often heard before the publication of *Paradise Lost*, and phrased on occasion with excessive zeal. The Italian philosopher Giordano Bruno, for instance, was convinced that a finite universe argues the absurd notion that God himself is finite and therefore imperfect; whereupon he maintained that 'as [God's] active power is infinite, so also as a necessary result,

the subject thereof is infinite' (*De l'Infinito Universo*, 1584; trans.
D. W. Singer, 1950). Not every scientist was prepared to accept some
of Bruno's wilder flights of fancy, and many recoiled from them in
horror. But the appropriateness of his quoted view to a poetic vision
of the universe did not escape Milton, especially in that the diffusion
of divine goodness within a world of measureless space powerfully
supports the 'great argument' of *Paradise Lost*.

Milton's Sources

The Renaissance was a period of spectacular achievements in nearly
every field of human endeavour. In England as on the Continent, the
exuberance of the age—and its recklessness—are best exemplified
in the labours of several representative individuals in particular.
Leonardo da Vinci (1452–1519) is possibly the most extravagant
example of the 'universal man' of the Renaissance, for he was not
only a great painter but at once an accomplished anatomist, philoso-
pher, musician, and engineer—while it is even said that he antici-
pated the sun-centred universe of Copernicus, the anatomical
discoveries of William Harvey, and the speculations of Newton on
gravity, and Einstein on time! The Count Pico della Mirandola
(1463–94) likewise accepted that his province was the universe, for
before his premature death he had already initiated a grandiose pro-
ject ambitiously aimed at welding human knowledge into a unified
whole. The same spirit appears to pervade the labours of many
individuals in England. Sir Walter Ralegh (1554–1618) once des-
cribed himself as 'a seafaring man, a soldier, and a courtier', but
he also composed poems, pursued commercial enterprises, designed
ships, dabbled in dietetics and naval medicine, and wrote a magis-
terial prose work significantly entitled The History of the World.
Sir Francis Bacon (1561–1626) with far greater consistency gave
himself to the task of revolutionising scientific methodology; for
even though he did not complete his vastly ambitious work, the
Instauratio Magna, yet 'he pointed along the road civilisation was to
take in the following centuries'.[1] By the time we come to Milton
(1608–74) we are not surprised to discover that some of his best
poems are in Latin, some of his sonnets in Italian, and a few of his
verses in Greek. Even more significantly, in prose he expostulated

[1] Douglas Bush, English Literature in the Earlier Seventeenth Century 2nd ed.
(1962), p. 275

at length on the freedom of the press, on divorce, and on the forms
of civil and ecclesiastical government, even as he wrote treatises on
education, grammar, logic, history, and theology. But it is worth
noting that Milton never looked on his literary endeavours as
enterprises in any way distinct from his responsibilities to society.
As he himself observed on one occasion, his ultimate ambition was
to advance the glory of God 'by the honour and instruction of my
country'.

Milton is particularly typical of the 'universal men' of the Renais-
sance in that he never wrote a major poem outside a given literary
tradition. *Comus* (first published in 1637) was composed within the
tradition of the masque; *Lycidas* (1638) is the culminating point of the
pastoral elegy; *Paradise Lost* (1667) is a direct descendant of Homer's
Iliad and Virgil's *Aeneid*; and *Samson Agonistes* (1671) is a tragedy in
imitation of Aeschylus, Sophocles and Euripides—'the three tragic
poets unequal'd yet by any', Milton pointedly reminds us. It is a
measure of Milton's achievement that a critic's description of *Lycidas*
as an 'unprecedented poem in which everything has a precedent',[1]
is no less applicable to his other poems, including *Paradise Lost*.
In other words, a study of the literary tradition to which *Paradise
Lost* belongs is of enormous value in our appreciation of the extent
to which the poem is similar to, and yet different from, its great
predecessors. Even as the similarities testify to the importance of the
literary echoes heard in *Paradise Lost*, so the differences direct our
attention to the significant ways that Milton altered the tradition of
epic poetry.[2] Accordingly, while the annotation of Milton's lines
in the present volume repeatedly calls attention to the importance

[1] B. Rajan, *The Lofty Rhyme* (1970) p. 49
[2] Despite the extensive scholarship available on Milton, there is no single
authoritative exposition of his classical heritage. But a good beginning has
been made by D. P. Harding in *Milton and the Renaissance Ovid* (1946) and
especially *The Club of Hercules: Studies in the Classical Background of 'Paradise
Lost'* (1962). See also C. M. Bowra's suggestive study of the changing epic
tradition in *From Virgil to Milton* (1948).

he attached to precedents, no reader of *Paradise Lost* could miss the
poet's sustained endeavour to discredit martial enterprises,

> hitherto the only argument
> Heroic deem'd, chief mastery to dissect
> With long and tedious havoc fabl'd knights
> In battles feign'd; the better fortitude
> Of patience and heroic martyrdom
> Unsung . . .
>
> (IX, 28–33)

Milton's Satan is firmly judged within the context of the epic
tradition as the exemplar of several 'heroic' qualities—but, signifi-
cantly, nothing more.

In so far as *Paradise Lost* is an epic poem, it is also a depository of the
vast knowledge which by definition falls within the province of the
epic. Aristotle's pronouncement in the fourth century BC that the
epic is inferior to tragedy (*Poetics*, Ch. 26) was inverted by Renais-
sance critics with almost total unanimity. As Sir Philip Sidney
proclaimed in his *Apology for Poetry* (1595), 'all concurreth to the
maintaining the heroical, which is not only a kind, but the best and
most accomplished kind of poetry'. Not only does it 'teach and move
to a truth', added Sidney, 'but teacheth and moveth to the most high
and excellent truth'—the universal truth which epic poetry alone
can encompass. Dryden's summary soon after the publication of
Paradise Lost echoes the tradition inherited by Milton himself: of an
epic poet 'who is worthy of that name, besides an universal genius,
is required universal learning'.

Milton's response to this challenge was to compress within
Paradise Lost a learning whose vast dimensions have been delineated
for us in several studies. His most important single source was, of
course, the Bible—but as amended (sometimes drastically) by hexae-
meral literature, i.e., the host of commentaries on the account of the

six days of creation in the Book of Genesis.[1] No less important were the traditional theological concepts as revised by Protestant authorities,[2] the scientific and pseudo-scientific lore current in the seventeenth century,[3] the aggregate of ideas relating to music,[4] and of course Greek and Roman mythology as interpreted by Christian expositors.[5] Finally, as if to provide Milton with a well-defined literary tradition within which he could display his talents, there were the numerous major literary treatments of man's creation and fall—including the relatively recent poems of du Bartas which in Joshua Sylvester's translation as *Divine Weekes and Workes* (first complete edition, 1608) were widely read in early seventeenth-century England; the Latin play *Adamus Exul* of Hugo Grotius (1601), and the Italian play *L'Adamo* of Giovanni Andreini (1613); and two rather late Dutch poems by Vondel.[6]

Milton asserts in *Paradise Lost* that the Bible is 'not but by the Spirit understood' (XII, 514). The degree to which his own fecund spirit tranformed the Biblical account of man's creation and/fall, however, should be obvious after reading the narrative in Genesis (Chapters 1–3). It is interesting to observe the way Milton enriches the

[1] The three basic studies are: M. I. Corcoran, *Milton's Paradise with Reference to the Hexameral Background* (1945); Arnold Williams, *The Common Expositor: An Account of the Commentaries on Genesis, 1527–1633* (1948); and J. M. Evans, *'Paradise Lost' and the Genesis Tradition* (1968).

[2] See C. A. Patrides, *Milton and the Christian Tradition* (1966).

[3] See Kester Svendsen, *Milton and Science* (1956). On the structure of the universe see E. M. W. Tillyard, *The Elizabethan World Picture* (1943), and the more sophisticated account by A. O. Lovejoy, *The Great Chain of Being* (1936).

[4] See John Hollander, *The Untuning of the Sky: Ideas of Music in English Poetry 1500–1700* (1961), and G. L. Finney, *Musical Backgrounds for English Literature 1580–1650* (1962).

[5] See Douglas Bush, *Mythology and the Renaissance Tradition in English Poetry* (rev. ed., 1962), The best work of reference is still C. G. Osgood, *The Classical Mythology of Milton's English Poems* (1900). See also above, page 219, note 2.

[6] Most of these works are available in part or in full in *The Celestial Cycle: The Theme of 'Paradise Lost' in World Literature with translations of the major analogues*, ed. Watson Kirkconnel (1952).

Biblical account even as he borrows or adapts the original phrasing for a particular effect.

CHAPTER 1

1 *In the beginning God created the heaven and the earth.*

2 *And the earth was without form, and void; and darkness was upon the face of the deep. And the Spirit of God moved upon the face of the waters.*

3 *And God said, Let there be light: and there was light.*

4 *And God saw the light, that it was good: and God divided the light from the darkness.*

5 *And God called the light Day, and the darkness he called Night. And the evening and the morning were the first day.*

6 *And God said, Let there be a firmament in the midst of the waters, and let it divide the waters from the waters.*

7 *And God made the firmament, and divided the waters which were under the firmament from the waters which were above the firmament: and it was so.*

8 *And God called the firmament Heaven. And the evening and the morning were the second day.*

9 *And God said, Let the waters under the heaven be gathered together unto one place, and let the dry land appear: and it was so.*

10 *And God called the dry land Earth; and the gathering together of the waters called he Seas: and God saw that it was good.*

11 *And God said, Let the earth bring forth grass, the herb yielding seed, and the fruit tree yielding fruit after his kind, whose seed is in itself, upon the earth: and it was so.*

12 *And the earth brought forth grass, and herb yielding seed after his kind, and the tree yielding fruit, whose seed was in itself, after his kind: and God saw that it was good.*

13 *And the evening and the morning were the third day.*

14 *And God said, Let there be lights in the firmament of the heaven to divide the day from the night; and let them be for signs, and for seasons, and for days, and years:*

15 *And let them be for lights in the firmament of the heaven to give light upon the earth: and it was so.*

16 *And God made two great lights; the greater light to rule the day, and the lesser light to rule the night; he made the stars also.*

17 *And God set them in the firmament of the heaven to give light upon the earth,*

18 *And to rule over the day and over the night, and to divide the light from the darkness: and God saw that it was good.*

19 *And the evening and the morning were the fourth day.*

20 *And God said, Let the waters bring forth abundantly the moving creature that hath life, and fowl that may fly above the earth in the open firmament of heaven.*

21 *And God created great whales, and every living creature that moveth, which the waters brought forth abundantly, after their kind, and every winged fowl after his kind: and God saw that it was good.*

22 *And God blessed them, saying, Be fruitful, and multiply, and fill the waters in the seas, and let fowl multiply in the earth.*

23 *And the evening and the morning were the fifth day.*

24 *And God said, Let the earth bring forth the living creature after his kind, cattle, and creeping thing, and beast of the earth after his kind: and it was so.*

25 *And God made the beast of the earth after his kind, and cattle after their kind, and everything that creepeth upon the earth after his kind: and God saw that it was good.*

26 *And God said, Let us make man in our image, after our likeness: and let them have dominion over the fish of the sea, and over the fowl of the air, and over the cattle, and over all the earth, and over every creeping thing that creepeth upon the earth.*

27 *So God created man in his own image, in the image of God created he him; male and female created he them.*

28 *And God blessed them, and God said unto them, Be fruitful, and multiply, and replenish the earth, and subdue it: and have dominion over the fish of the sea, and over the fowl of the air, and over every living thing that moveth upon the earth.*

29 *And God said, Behold, I have given you every herb bearing seed, which is upon the face of all the earth, and every tree, in the which is the fruit of a tree yielding seed; to you it shall be for meat.*

30 *And to every beast of the earth, and to every fowl of the air, and to every thing that creepeth upon the earth, wherein there is life, I have given every green herb for meat: and it was so.*

31 *And God saw every thing that he had made, and, behold, it was very good. And the evening and the morning were the sixth day.*

CHAPTER 2

1 *Thus the heavens and the earth were finished, and all the host of them.*

2 *And on the seventh day God ended his work which he had made; and he rested on the seventh day from all his work which he had made.*

3 *And God blessed the seventh day, and sanctified it: because that in it he had rested from all his work which God created and made.*

4 *These are the generations of the heavens and of the earth when they were created, in the day that the Lord God made the earth and the heavens,*

5 *And every plant of the field before it was in the earth, and every herb of the field before it grew: for the Lord God had not caused it to rain upon the earth, and there was not a man to till the ground.*

6 *But there went up a mist from the earth, and watered the whole face of the ground.*

7 *And the Lord God formed man of the dust of the ground, and breathed into his nostrils the breath of life; and man become a living soul.*

8 *And the Lord God planted a garden eastward in Eden: and there he put the man whom he had formed.*

9 *And out of the ground made the Lord God to grow every tree that is pleasant to the sight, and good for food; the tree of life also in the midst of the garden, and the tree of knowledge of good and evil.*

10 *And a river went out of Eden to water the garden; and from thence it was parted, and became into four heads.*

11 *The name of the first is Pison: that is it which compasseth the whole land of Havilah, where there is gold;*

12 *And the gold of the land is good: there is bdellium and the onyx stone.*

13 *And the name of the second river is Gihon: the same is it that compasseth the whole land of Ethiopia.*

14 *And the name of the third river is Hiddekel: that is it which goeth toward the east of Assyria. And the fourth river is Euphrates.*

15 *And the Lord God took the man, and put him into the garden of Eden to dress it and to keep it.*

16 *And the Lord God commanded the man, saying, Of every tree of the garden thou mayest freely eat:*

17 *But of the tree of the knowledge of good and evil, thou shalt not eat of it: for in the day that thou eatest thereof thou shalt surely die.*

18 *And the Lord God said, It is not good that the man should be alone; I will make him an help meet for him.*

19 *And out of the ground the Lord God formed every beast of the field, and every fowl of the air; and brought them unto Adam to see what he would call them: and whatsoever Adam called every living creature, that was the name thereof.*

20 *And Adam gave names to all cattle, and to the fowl of the air, and to every beast of the field; but for Adam there was not found an help meet for him.*

21 *And the Lord God caused a deep sleep to fall upon Adam, and he slept: and he took one of his ribs, and closed up the flesh instead thereof;*

22 *And the rib, which the Lord God had taken from man, made he a woman, and brought her unto the man.*

23 *And Adam said, This is now bone of my bones, and flesh of my flesh: she shall be called Woman, because she was taken out of Man.*

24 *Therefore shall a man leave his father and his mother, and shall cleave unto his wife: and they shall be one flesh.*

25 *And they were both naked, the man and his wife, and were not ashamed.*

CHAPTER 3

1 *Now the serpent was more subtil than any beast of the field which the Lord God had made. And he said unto the woman, Yea, hath God said, Ye shall not eat of every tree of the garden?*

2 *And the woman said unto the serpent, We may eat of the fruit of the trees of the garden:*

3 *But of the fruit of the tree which is in the midst of the garden, God hath said, Ye shall not eat of it, neither shall ye touch it, lest ye die.*

4 *And the serpent said unto the woman, Ye shall not surely die:*

5 *For God doth know that in the day ye eat thereof, then your eyes shall be opened, and ye shall be as gods, knowing good and evil.*

6 *And when the woman saw that the tree was good for food, and that it was pleasant to the eyes, and a tree to be desired to make one wise, she took of the fruit thereof, and did eat, and gave also unto her husband with her; and he did eat.*

7 *And the eyes of them both were opened, and they knew that they were naked; and they sewed fig leaves together, and made themselves aprons.*

8 *And they heard the voice of the Lord God walking in the garden in the cool of the day; and Adam and his wife hid themselves from the presence of the Lord God amongst the trees of the garden.*

9 *And the Lord God called unto Adam, and said unto him, Where art thou?*

10 *And he said, I heard thy voice in the garden, and I was afraid, because I was naked; and I hid myself.*

11 *And he said, Who told thee that thou wast naked? Hast thou eaten of the tree, whereof I commanded thee that thou shouldest not eat?*

12 *And the man said, The woman whom thou gavest to be with me, she gave me of the tree, and I did eat.*

13 *And the Lord God said unto the woman, What is this that thou hast done? And the woman said, The serpent beguiled me, and I did eat.*

14 *And the Lord God said unto the serpent, Because thou hast done this, thou art cursed above all cattle, and above every beast of the field; upon thy belly shalt thou go, and dust shalt thou eat all the days of thy life:*

15 *And I will put enmity between thee and the woman, and between thy seed and her seed; it shall bruise thy head, and thou shalt bruise his heel.*

16 *Unto the woman he said, I will greatly multiply thy sorrow and thy conception; in sorrow thou shalt bring forth children; and thy desire shalt be to thy husband, and he shall rule over thee.*

17 *And unto Adam he said, Because thou hast hearkened unto the voice of thy wife, and hast eaten of the tree, of which I commanded thee, saying, Thou shalt not eat of it: cursed is the ground for thy sake; in sorrow shalt thou eat of it all the days of thy life;*

18 *Thorns also and thistles shall it bring forth to thee; and thou shalt eat the herb of the field;*

19 *In the sweat of thy face shalt thou eat bread, till thou return unto the ground; for out of it wast thou taken: for dust thou art, and unto dust shalt thou return.*

20 *And Adam called his wife's name Eve; because she was the mother of all living.*

21 *Unto Adam also and to his wife did the Lord God make coats of skins, and clothed them.*

22 *And the Lord God said, Behold, the man is become as one of us, to know good and evil: and now, lest he put forth his hand, and take also of the tree of life, and eat, and live for ever:*

23 *Therefore the Lord God sent him forth from the garden of Eden, to till the ground from whence he was taken.*

24 *So he drove out the man; and he placed at the east of the garden of Eden cherubims, and a flaming sword which turned every way, to keep the way of the tree of life.*

Reading List

Several annual bibliographies list the latest studies of Milton: the English Association's *The Year's Work in English Studies*; the Modern Humanities Research Association's *Annual Bibliography of English Language and Literature*; *Publications of the Modern Language Association of America; Studies in Philology;* and *Milton Quarterly.* There are comprehensive bibliographies in Douglas Bush, *English Literature in the Earlier Seventeenth Century* (Oxford, 2nd rev. ed., 1962), and C. A. Patrides, ed., *Milton's Epic Poetry* (Penguin Books, 1967).

The standard edition is *The Works of John Milton*, gen. ed. F. A. Patterson (1931–40), 20 vols.; in part being superseded by the scholarly edition of the *Complete Prose Works of John Milton*, gen. ed. D. M. Wolfe (1953 ff.), 7 vols. There are fully annotated one-volume editions of the poetry by M. Y. Hughes (1957), Douglas Bush (1966), John Carey and A. D. S. Fowler (1968), *et al*.

The best critical biographies of Milton are by E. M. W. Tillyard (1930), J. H. Hanford (1949), David Daiches (1957), Emile Saillens (1959, translated 1964), and Douglas Bush(1964). The most magisterial work is W. R. Parker's *Milton: A Biography* (1968), 2 vols. All the accounts rely on The *Early Lives of Milton* ed. Helen Darbishire (1932).

On the Age of Milton

Bush, Douglas, *The Renaissance and English Humanism* (1939)
Haller, William, *The Rise of Puritanism* (1938)
Willey, Basil, *The Seventeenth Century Background* (1934)
Wolfe, D. M., *Milton in the Puritan Revolution* (1934)

On Milton's Thought

Brinkley, R. F., *Arthurian Legend in the 17th Century* (1932). On Milton's gradual revision of his plans for an epic, pp. 126–41.
Hughes, M. Y., *Ten Perspectives on Milton* (1965)
Patrides, C. A., *Milton and the Christian Tradition* (1966)
Steadman, J. M., *Milton and the Renaissance Hero* (1967)
Svendsen, Kester, *Milton and Science* (1956)
Tillyard, E. M. W., *The English Epic and its Background* (1954)

On Milton's Versification

Langdon, Ida, *Milton's Theory of Poetry and Fine Art* (1924)
Sprott, S. E., *Milton's Art of Prosody* (1953)
Watkins, W. B. C., *An Anatomy of Milton's Verse* (1955)

Discussions of 'Paradise Lost'

(1) Introductory

Diekhoff, J. S., *Milton's 'Paradise Lost': A Commentary on the Argument* (1945)
Frye, Northrop, *Five Essays on Milton's Epics* (1966)
Lewis, C. S., *A Preface to 'Paradise Lost'* (1942)
Nicolson, M. H., *A Reader's Guide to John Milton* (1964)
Rudrum, Alan, *Milton: 'Paradise Lost'* (1966)
Wright, B. A., *Milton's 'Paradise Lost'* (1962)

(2) Advanced

Broadbent, J. B., *Some Graver Subject* (1960)
Eliot, T. S., *Milton: Two Essays* (1968), originally published in 1936 and 1947, respectively
Empson, William, *Milton's God* (rev. ed., 1965)

Gardner, Helen, *A Reading of 'Paradise Lost'* (1965)
Prince, F. T., *The Italian Element in Milton's Verse* (1954)
Rajan, B., *The Lofty Rhyme* (1970)
Ricks, Christopher, *Milton's Grand Style* (1963)
Stein, Arnold, *Answerable Style* (1953)
Summers, J. H., *The Muse's Method* (1962)

Collections of Essays

Barker, A. E. (ed.), *Milton: Modern Essays in Criticism* (1965)
Critical Essays on Milton from ELH (1969)
Emma, R. D., and Shawcross, J. T. (eds.), *Language and Style in Milton* (1967)
Kermode, F. (ed.), *The Living Milton* (1960)
Martz, L. L. (ed.), *'Paradise Lost': A Collection of Critical Essays* (1966)
Patrides, C. A. (ed.), *Approaches to 'Paradise Lost'* (1968)
Patrides, C. A. (ed.), *Milton's Epic Poetry: Essays on 'Paradise Lost' and 'Paradise Regained'* (1967)
Rudrum, A. (ed.), *Milton: Modern Judgements* (1968)
Stein, A. (ed.), *On Milton's Poetry: A Selection of Modern Studies* (1970)
Thorpe, J. (ed.), *Milton Criticism: Selections from Four Centuries* (1950)

On Milton's Illustrators

Baker, C. H. C., 'Some Illustrators of Milton's *Paradise Lost* (1688–1850)', *Library*, 5th series, III (1948), 1–21, 101–19
Baker, C. H. C., 'William Blake, Painter', *Huntington Library Bulletin*, X (1936), 135–48
Gardner, Helen, 'Milton's First Illustrator [i.e. J. B. Medina]', *Essays and Studies*, new series, IX (1956), 27–38
Pointon, Marcia R., *Milton and English Art* (1970)
Trapp, J. B., 'The Iconography of the Fall of Man', *Approaches to 'Paradise Lost'*, ed. C. A. Patrides (1968). The best study of the iconographic background.